An Officer's Wife in Ireland

An Officer's Wife in Ireland

Parkgate Publications Ltd:

2 Parkfield Avenue	19 Montague Street
London SW14 8DY	Dublin 2
England	Ireland
Tel: 081 878 7402	Tel: 01 475 8778

ISBN: 0-9523109-1-0

Printed by Colour Books Ltd

Publisher's Note

Originally published by William Blackwood & Sons under the title *Experiences of An Officer's Wife in Ireland,* this book has been re-edited and augmented with previously classified War Office material. Authorship of the original work, which was published anonymously in 1921, has been difficult to ascertain. None the less, on the basis of contemporary newspaper reports, it has been possible to determine the identity of the principal characters of the book. The Officer's Wife of the title is Caroline Woodcock, who was born in the Channel Islands in 1886. She was married to Lt. Col. Wilfrid James Woodcock, who was among the British casualties on Bloody Sunday 1920. Lt. Col. Woodcock subsequently went on to command a battalion of the Home Guard in the Second World War and died in 1960. Mrs Woodcock died in London at the age of 85, a fortnight after the January 1972 Bloody Sunday shootings in Northern Ireland.

Despite the incorporation of some additional material and the use of illustrations for the first time, this new revised edition remains faithful to the original account of the events in Ireland at the time.

An Officer's Wife in Ireland

Contents

List of Illustrations

Illustrations by David Oliver

INTRODUCTION

One man's - or woman's - freedom fighter is another's terrorist. The point, which still has resonances for Anglo-Irish relationships today, comes across very clearly in this memoir of a British officer's wife, thought to be Caroline Woodcock, who had the unenviable distinction of being a witness to the Bloody Sunday assassinations of November 21st 1920.

From the point of view of the IRA, these were a coup of coups, the ferocious counter-punch with which Michael Collins destroyed the British Intelligence effort that had come within an ace of crippling his guerilla offensive. In all nearly a score of officers were shot, many in the presence of their wives and mistresses. A lucky few survived their wounds, including the husband of this memorialist. Her, very different, British perception of the incident, as traumatic as it was pivotal, was naturally heightened by his ordeal. A brave man, who was shot twice, he told his wife before lapsing into unconsciousness:

"It's all right darling, they have only hit outlying portions of me."

There is a poignant contrast between the officer's valour, his wife's consequential honest outrage, and the cynicism with which their Prime Minister Lloyd George received the news of the deaths:

"... they got what they deserved - beaten by counter-jumpers." [1]

For, just as has happened so often in our day, the British Government had been relying for the solution to their Irish difficulties on a military approach to what was essentially a political problem. Prevented by both domestic and world opinion from attempting a full-blooded military onslaught, a coalition Liberal-Conservative Cabinet had shrunk from a political initiative, in the face of Conservative and Unionist intransigence, and opted instead for the concept of a "police war".

Special forces were recruited. These were the Black and Tans, drawn from the ranks of ex-servicemen, and a corps of ex-officers, the Auxiliary Police Cadets. Their ostensible brief was to aid the police in combating Sinn Fein, the precursor of today's eponymous organisation, which was portrayed, not as a national movement, but as a criminal gang of murderers. In practice an unacknowledged "shoot-to-kill" policy was inaugurated, to which the Government turned a blind eye, refusing to take any responsibility for reprisals as Field Marshal Sir Henry Wilson has noted in his Diary.[2]

The reprisal strategy, with which Northern Ireland is once again familiar today, relied, as Wilson has recorded[3], on intelligence agents who:

> "... marked down certain SFs as in their opinion the actual murderers or instigators and coolly went out and shot them without question or trial."

In Dublin a key unit involved in the fingering, and often the killings of "SFs", was the "Cairo Gang", so called because some of the officers involved had been active in Middle Eastern Intelligence, and because members of the group frequented Dublin's Cairo Cafe. These men, who generally did not live in barracks, often operated after dark, under cover of curfew, with blackened faces, wearing rubber-soled shoes and in civilian clothing.

Mrs Woodcock attributes the civilian clothing to reasons of hygiene, rather than a desire to escape identification. She writes:

"... some of the descriptions given to me by officers, to whose unhappy lot had fallen the searching of some of the filthy tenement houses in which Dublin slums abound make me quite ill... five or six in a bed was quite usual, imagine searching such a bed and pulling the mattress to pieces ... a few days in hospital subsequent to a raid such as this, to get rid of a complaint common amongst the great unwashed, were often necessary."

She does not mention the Cairo Gang, nor the overall political situation, and appears unaware that her husband's nocturnal activities might literally have had a darker side:

"In Dublin both officers and men rather welcomed a raid ...There was always the hope of a scrap, of getting a little of their own back. When volunteers were called for, the whole regiment[4] usually responded. Dressed in filthy old clothes and rubber soled shoes, especially kept for what was frequently very dirty work, they sallied forth in parties of twenty or so, with one or more officers ...

"On these occasions my husband would come back to our flat about tea-time as usual. He would stay for dinner, and then about 9 o'clock would suddenly announce that he was going out again, and that he would not be back that night. He was always afraid that a chance word would arouse the suspicions of the Irish servants."

However the Irish servants learned enough about Woodcock and the other occupants of his supposedly safe house, No. 28 Upper Pembroke St., Dublin, to alert Michael Collins. On Bloody Sunday, November 21st 1920, six officers billeted at the address were among those shot that day, three of them fatally. A vital element in Lloyd George's Irish strategy had been destroyed.

Caroline Woodcock does not use the term "Bloody". It was considered impolite. Instead she talks about "Red Sunday". Nor does she allude to the reprisals which followed the shooting of her husband and his colleagues. The Black and Tans and the Auxiliaries machine-gunned a football crowd at Croke Park, killing fourteen civilians and wounding hundreds more. In Dublin Castle three prisoners, one of them innocent of Sinn Fein involvement, the other two close associates of Michael Collins, were tortured to death.

And of course she completely ignores the significance of the officers' deaths for the British counter-insurgency effort. Nevertheless, though condescending and dismissive about Ireland, which she initially loved and romanticised from afar, through the writings of Somerville and Ross, this spirited woman has left a valuable picture of what it was like for someone of her now bygone class to live through those last days of British rule in Dublin.

The present publisher is to be commended on rescuing this work from oblivion. The original publisher has vanished, as have virtually all of the Woodcock descendants. Only an interview in the *Irish Times* on November 24th, 1920 corroborates the fact that Caroline witnessed the Bloody Sunday shootings. The book was first published in July 1921, but overlooked in the euphoria surrounding the Truce which it was hoped had ended Anglo-Irish hostilities in that month. The Treaty that followed ushered in today's Ireland. Unfortunately the euphoria has long since vanished but the Bloody Sundays remain. *An Officer's Wife* illustrates some facets of the reasons why.

Tim Pat Coogan,
Dublin,
February, 1994

[1] *Michael Collins*, by Tim Pat Coogan, pg. 187 (Arrow, London, 1991)

[2] *Diaries of Field Marshall Sir Henry Wilson*, ed. C.E. Calwell, entry for 29/9/1920 (Cassell, London, 1927)

[3] Ibid., 23/9/1920

[4] Woodcock's regiment was the 1st Lancashire Fusiliers, which was quartered in a disused Dublin workhouse, the North Dublin Union.

CHAPTER I

HOUSE-HUNTING

I LEFT IRELAND a few days ago, for ever. I motored from Dublin to Kingstown in an armoured car. An armed escort brought me to London, where Scotland Yard took charge of me, and I hope are looking after me still.

However, when I arrived in Ireland I did not know what the manner of my departure would be, and it was indeed a case of "where ignorance is bliss." My husband had gone over in March, soon after we had left Germany. On 4th March he was at the War Office, and was told he and his regiment, the 1st Lancashire Fusiliers, would shortly go back to India; on 5th March he was ordered to Ireland. They both began with "I," which was the only way that we could account for the mistake, but alas! it was not a mistake. In recent years, the regiment had seen service in South Africa, India, the Middle East, France and latterly Germany. Within a few weeks of receiving their orders, two dozen officers and some 1,150 other ranks arrived at Dublin's North Wall from Aldershot.

I followed him in July. I had utterly refused to stay away

any longer, and refused also to be daunted or depressed by the dismal reports I received from my husband and other officers and their wives who were there already, one officer going so far as to head his letter to me with the address "B——y Dublin." Had I not been brought up on Irish hunting books, was I not prepared to love the country and the people, and was it not only a question of a few months before I too should be hunting in Ireland? At last I should meet some of the characters I read about so often in the 'Irish R.M.' and many other delightful books. I certainly did see a man once who looked like "Slipper," otherwise I never saw, met or heard of any one who in the least resembled any of the characters in those books. Another illusion gone.

Before leaving London I was taken by a friend to a literary meeting in Chelsea. I was told the President of the Society was a delightful Irishwoman, and that she was certain to talk about Ireland and Sinn Fein. I was very keen to hear something about the other, or Sinn Fein, side. I knew once I got to Dublin I should only hear and see the military point of view, and I was genuinely interested in the Sinn Feiners, and had a good deal of sympathy with them.

The lady was a disappointment: she certainly compared England most unfavourably with Ireland, and if you like to be amused at the expense of your own country, she was amusing. Like all the Irish people I have ever met, she dilated on the wit, gaiety, beauty, &c., of the Irish nation. But all that was neither interesting nor enlightening. As I was leaving, to my embarrassment, she drew me to her and kissed me [mere Irish impulsiveness, I suppose], and said: "Come back and tell me all about it, if they do not knock you on the head."

I laughed at her little jest; I did not laugh when that jest nearly became reality.

The Irish Channel was very kind. The boat, a big new

one, was a great deal more comfortable than many I had travelled on to India. I arrived at Kingstown in a frame of mind ready to be pleased with everything and everybody. That condition lasted about one hour. The taxi ordered to meet me had not arrived. I found out afterwards that taxis ordered by military people seldom, if ever, did arrive, and as I drove in a dirty cab through the filthy Dublin streets my heart sank.

Our soldier servant was waiting for us at the hotel. He was an old friend, and I remarked to him that I did not think I should like the place very much. He replied: "We must just make the best of it, madam." He made the best of it by deserting the next day in a blue-serge suit belonging to my husband! I envied him, but alas, he would redeem himself at a later stage.

I started off the next morning to look for a flat. The house-agent was gloomy and not particularly helpful. In some ways he was just like his English *confrères*. He had the same powerful imagination, the same peculiarly annoying habit of sending one on long and fruitless journeys after flats that either had been let three months ago, or else had never been to let at all. He asked me how long I wanted it for, so I answered brightly for as long as the troops remain in Dublin. He replied that would be for ever, and became gloomier still. He told me the rent of one particular flat was £9 a week. It seemed a good deal, and I said I would go and look at it. As I was going out of the door he told me it might be £9 a month. I asked facetiously if he was sure that it was not £9 a year. But, as I often noticed, no Irishman ever sees a joke unless he had made it himself, and not always then.

There were not many flats to look at. Dublin was very full, not only of military, but of lots of people who had places in the country and who had been frightened out of them by one side or the other, and were now living in Dublin.

At last I found a house in Fitzwilliam Square, one of the

best squares in Dublin. It looked promising from the outside at any rate. On entering the hall, though, there was a faint smell which reminded me somehow of Malta. I sniffed again; what was it? I suddenly remembered. Surely I was mistaken?

At that moment the servant came back, and with her was a goat. I had not been mistaken: no one who has ever lived in Malta could ever forget that smell. I suppose I looked, as I felt, astonished, as the girl smiled and said: "He is generally in the house." I had heard that pigs lived in Irish cabins, but I had never heard that goats lived in Irish flats. However, the goat, though a large one, was but a small shock to the one I was presently to receive.

A lady stood in the dining-room, and I explained that I had heard she had a flat to let furnished, and could I see it. I suppose she was struck by what she would call my "English accent," as before answering she asked sternly: "Who are you?" I told her, hoping that my husband's official position would vouch both for my respectability and ability to pay the rent.

There was a silence, and then to my utter amazement she said: "How dare you come into my house!" and then a torrent of words, mostly unintelligible. I stared at her in utter speechless amazement. All I could think of was that she was evidently quite mad, and how was I to get to the door? But after a few minutes, when she paused for breath, I realised that here was one of the people I had wanted so much to meet - a Sinn Feiner - and that she was not mad, or at least only mad on one subject, England and the English.

I had only been twenty-four hours in Ireland. I had not the faintest idea that any one hated us, and that I, as the wife of an officer, was a special object of hatred. No one had ever hated me in Germany.

I had started off that morning to look for a flat in Dublin in exactly the same way as I would have gone out in London. Then I suddenly found myself in the house of a woman who described herself as "England's bitterest enemy." When she got calmer I asked her if she would explain things to me, as I honestly wanted to understand the situation. She told me a great deal about Ireland under Cromwell and Lord French, and of General Dyer's methods in India; she evidently classed them together, and spoke of all three in the same breath with equal bitterness. She then told me that she had prayed to God every night of the war that He would let Germany win, and she was now praying to Him to take the soldiers away from Ireland.

I was rather bored by this time, and said that I hoped for my own sake that her present prayers would be more successful than her previous one, and prepared to go. She escorted me to the door, still talking. I felt safer in the hall, and ventured a remark about Ulster, and how, though Irish, they had fought for England.

"Ulster," she replied in tones of contempt, "Ulster is England, so, of course the Ulstermen had fought; but had not lots of Irish boys fought too?" - though she had personally gone down on her knees to implore them not to.

This lady then asked me why my husband had come to Dublin - "a fine soldier he must be, to do this coward's work." I could not think of any reason except that he was a soldier; we certainly had not come for pleasure. I was asked why the English Government, who used to send clever men to govern Ireland, now only send fools. This, and similar questions, I could not answer, and suddenly the humour of it all struck me, and I began to laugh. But, poor lady, it was no laughing matter to her.

We eventually parted friends, and she told me that I should be quite safe in Dublin, but did not seem so sure about my husband, and I left her with her goat.

I tried one more flat in the same square. But before entering, warned by my previous experience, I asked the lady if she objected to officers. This landlady was kinder. She did, and she did not object - any way I might look around. No, she was not exactly loyal; she was neutral, I gathered, with a strong leaning towards Sinn Fein. Unfortunately this flat had little or no furniture in it. It was indescribably dirty. Kitchen there was none. She said she used the cupboard and an oil-stove. I asked for a bathroom, and was told there was a tap on the landing. I thought of my beautiful bathrooms in Germany, with their tiled floors and walls, their endless array of taps, sprays, showers, and douches. Here I was offered a tap on the landing; and once more I was overcome with laughter.

Murmuring something about coming back with my husband, I fled. I could not help seeing the funny side of it all.

Those first few months in Ireland were a mixture of comedy and tragedy, until the tragedy came which blotted out all the comedy in a sea of blood, and made me feel that I could never smile at anything Irish again.

Eventually, a day or two later, I did get a very nice service flat, in a house in Upper Pembroke-street, where there were eight or nine suites of rooms, several of them already occupied by officers and their wives, and others by six or seven men who shared rooms. I never quite knew what those men were, and I wondered if they were officers why they did not live in barracks. Two, we were told were in the Ordnance, and the others we knew as "the Hush Hush men." They came in and went out at odd hours, and I never really got to know any of them. Most of them are now dead.

I told an officer in the Intelligence Service of my amusing experience while house-hunting, and gave the name and address of the lady in Fitzwilliam Square. He told me she was a well-known rebel, and that the troops had raided her house several times.

I was never quite sure if it had been altogether amusing.

It was a novel experience to be hated and told so. I realised just a little the intense hatred with which the English are regarded by a large majority of Irish men and women, a hatred which no one in England ever believes in or even tries to understand. If that feeling existed then, seven or eight months ago, it must be a thousand times intensified now, when tragedy after tragedy has occurred to inflame the passions of both sides.

It is because I know that feeling exists, and because it was brought forcibly home to me by another woman my very first day in Ireland, that I personally can see no end to the present appalling position. They have not forgiven England yet for Cromwell's deeds. Perhaps when another 250 years have passed they will have forgotten Cromwell; but when another officer's wife goes house-hunting in Dublin in the year 2170 (for, like my house-agent friend, I also think there will be troops in Ireland for ever), doubtless that wife will be met with a long account of the misdeeds of Lord French and Sir Nevil Macready, for time does not soften things in that unhappy country.

CHAPTER II

TYPES

I DO NOT think any one has ever written anything about Ireland without alluding, at least once, to the Dublin Metropolitan Police, and I cannot resist the temptation either. They are all so big, so beautiful, and so unutterably stupid. As one approaches the fashionable part of Dublin, they get larger and handsomer in every street. One particularly beautiful specimen stood at the top of Grafton-street, the Bond-street of Dublin, and was a well-known landmark. A friend of mine, if asked whether she was going out that morning, would reply, "I shall just stroll up Grafton-street and look at the policeman, and then home again." He was certainly well worth looking at. Towards the river, they tail off a little. However, I found it was useless to ask them the simplest question. They smiled quite delightfully, but seldom knew the name of the street at the corner of which they were standing. The destinations of the various trams were a sealed book to them, and I am sure they never knew the time.

One half of Dublin seems to live by selling newspapers to

the other half. With horrid yells, boys and men dashed down the street several times a day with special editions. There was always something to sell the papers: rumours of agreements with England, conflicts between the police or military and the I.R.A., the almost daily murders.

The posters of these Irish newspapers were often amusing reading as they displayed such marvellous ingenuity. I am sure that, during the Kidwell murder trial, countless people in Ireland believed, as they were intended to believe, that it was the Irish Secretary who was on trial for the murder of his wife. Huge placards appeared, "H. Greenwood on trial for his life." "Did Greenwood poison his wife?" To the untutored it might be natural to confuse Sir Hamar with his namesake on trial, Harold Greenwood.

I felt quite sorry for the papers during the last few weeks of the Cork hunger-strike. For the first month the posters were pathetic and moving; later they felt the strain. It was a long time, and to find something fresh daily was evidently difficult.

The other inhabitants of Dublin which made the most impression on me - literally, indeed - were the fleas. Never have I known such animals. The Italian and Spanish varieties, which I had already encountered, paled into insignificance before these monsters. I never went on a tram without returning with one or more of these creatures, and I never faced the theatre in Dublin, as I was warned I should be eaten alive if I did.

Fortunately, I personally escaped the other perils. One poor lady told me in an awestruck whisper that, after going on one particularly filthy tram, which we all knew well, she had found "one of those things the men had in the trenches."

I do not think that even Dublin's admirers - and I do not count myself among them - would deny its dirt and its beggars. The beauty of its children is undeniable, at least as far as you can see it for dirt. The beggars nearly drove me distracted; they all looked at the last stage of destitution, and they were so horribly persistent, following one for quite long distances, whining and flattering. They missed many a penny from me, though, by calling me a "lovely lady with Irish eyes," or "you might be Irish yourself now" - another favourite remark - which doubtless well-meant compliments, had they but known it, were the invariable signal for me to put my money back in my pocket. Since I have a Scotch background, I consider myself Scotch and I glory in the fact. I detested being told I looked Irish. Probably they would have been equally disgusted if I had told them that they looked Scotch.

The horses were the nicest things I saw in Dublin. I was always too busy holding on when I was on an outside car to admire them, but safely in the street again, I could, and did, realise what extraordinarily good and well-kept animals some of them were.

The drivers were a curious mixture. Once, in a hoarse whisper, I was told by one old gentleman that he was afraid of the Sinn Feiners himself. He had warned a member of the R.I.C. of an attempted plot against him, and how he was terrified out of his life for fear he would be shot himself. Whether this was really true, or whether he merely hoped to get an extra tip out of me by his pathetic story, I do not know. Anyway, he got his shilling.

Once, on my way to our stables, I gave the horse a bit of the sugar I was taking to my own mare, at the same time asking the driver, "Is your horse a Sinn Feiner too?" Without a moment's hesitation he replied, "Yes, indeed, my lady."

I always used to tell the driver where I wanted to go before getting on to the car, as often, after I had climbed laboriously up and given directions, "The Castle" or "The Royal Hospital," I was told to get down again. They would not take you to these hated places. I always felt furious, but there was nothing for it but to climb ignominiously down and try again.

Other people find so much in the Irish to amuse them. I only found them funny when they were unconsciously so.

There was a dear old lady who occupied a flat in our house, who was a perpetual source of amusement to me. She started our first conversation by telling me she had a castle. Most Irish people have, I fancy; they are always talking about them. I only have one lot of friends in England who have a castle, and they are only too thankful if they can let it, furnished, at five guineas a week. But in Ireland they take their castles more seriously.

This old lady was always indicating to me - unconsciously, I am sure - how very superior she, as a member of an old Irish family with castle complete, was to every one else. Once when I told her I was going to a dance at Dublin Castle, she said, "A very mixed affair, I expect." I replied meekly that, as it was only for military people, it probably would be mixed.

Another time, when I returned from a fortnight in England, she asked me what my friends in England were saying about Ireland. I truthfully replied, "Literally nothing, as far as I can see, no one ever talks, or wants to hear anything at all about Ireland." She said, "Oh, that would be just among the bourgeoisie, I suppose." But, though struggling with laughter, I could not help murmuring that all my friends were not "among the bourgeoisie." This same old lady had two sons in the British Army, but she was an ardent Sinn Feiner, and had many and varied grievances against the British Government. Some of her remarks on that subject I really dare not reproduce.

One day I said something about the coming Christmas in Dublin. "Christmas in Dublin," she replied; "surely all the troops will have gone long before that." I said I sincerely hoped so, but that it seemed very unlikely - and added, "You know if we do all go, you and your friends will probably be murdered," and repeated the formula I had heard so often that it was only the troops who stood between Ireland and civil war. "Well," she said, "leave us to be murdered; can't we even murder each other without England interfering?"

But a few weeks later, when murder was done in that very house, this old lady lay on the floor in her room. She explained that she had heard that this was the safest thing to do in an air-raid. Not that there had ever been any air-raids in Ireland, of course. She was so terribly frightened when I saw her, that I took her up to a lovely Dublin Metropolitan policeman, whom I had found standing aimlessly in the hall. I thought he might be a comfort to her.

I met another very characteristic Irish lady at Dublin Castle one day. I was having tea with an official there, and she had come to complain about her own castle. It was not being property treated, she said, by the Auxiliaries, or Black and Tans, as she called them, who were billeted there. When she was introduced to my husband and myself, she said severely, "There are far too many military people here." I felt the same so replied, "I quite agree with you; at least there are two too many."

Afterwards, when my husband was nearly killed, hers was the first message of sympathy that I received. She was genuinely and utterly horrified at the murders. She felt for us with her whole heart. I think she was typical of many. She had three great loves - Ireland as one nation, the British Empire [though *not* the British Government], and the Royal Irish Constabulary.

But there were three things she hated as much as she loved the others. They were - the Germans, Ulster, and the Black and Tans. The last Home Rule Bill she utterly condemned as dividing Ireland in two. But, though she declared herself an ardent Home Ruler, she did not state how she proposed to reconcile her hatred for Ulster with Ireland as one nation. I have repeated her conversation almost word for word. She bears a name which is known throughout Ireland. She has great wealth and a great position, and I found much food for thought in her remarks, but no solution of the problem - her statements were so hopelessly inconsistent, her feelings so irreconcilable. And I am certain she is only one of many who love as she loves, hate as she hates, and whose loves and hates are daily getting further apart. But I do not propose to discuss politics or religion in these pages. The two are, to a great extent, one in Ireland. I think what I most want to write about is the British Army.

I have always understood that Cromwell, of whom I heard so much in Dublin, founded our Army. I can only wonder that Ireland has not finished it. It was Cromwell who said that soldiers ought to be "men who make some conscience of what they do; men who know what they are fighting for, and love what they know." I only know from hearsay of the deeds, chivalry, self-sacrifice, and devotion to duty of our men in France and in the other theatres of war. But what I did see with my own eyes in Ireland was the same devotion to duty, discipline, and cheerful obedience to orders under the most hateful and disagreeable circumstances: the same never-failing courtesy and good temper under the greatest provocation. Only once did I see them otherwise. And these are the men and boys, we are told, who murder and rob the innocent and peaceful inhabitants, and burn unoffending villages wholesale. In every other country in the world in which he has fought, except Ireland, the British Tommy has made friends. He bears no malice, and he is quite unable to hit a man when he is down.

A great deal of the soldier's work in Dublin is done at night. He is often short of sleep, the strain on his nerves is appalling, but he never fails, never loses patience. All the horrible work he has to do is carried out with kindness and consideration. But how he despises and hates the inhabitants! I read in the papers one day that they were letting out five hundred of the less dangerous lunatics from the asylums, as they could no longer afford to feed them. I remarked on this to one of our sergeants. "Well, they won't be noticed among all the other lunatics," was his only comment.

Even the soldier servants, who came daily to our flats to clean the boots and uniforms of the various officers, refused to do their work in the same room as the Irish servants. They preferred not to mix with them at all, and cleaned and polished on the landings. Two or three of these Irish servants openly said they hated us; the others were civil and obliging - far more so than most English servants - and they never seemed to mind how much they ran up and down the stairs. [In fact, I wonder where the murderers of 21st November got their accurate knowledge of the house. They knew who occupied each room, they made no mistakes, and wasted no time.]

One Irish friend who came through Dublin on her way to her home in Limerick told me of the extraordinary vindictiveness of the people there. Her brother had joined the Army, and had been killed in the war. The family had lived in the neighbourhood for generations, and everybody knew them. Yet the sole remark of an old man who worked on the estate, when told of this boy's death in action, was, "A good thing too; one dirty traitor the less."

Another lady told me that her daughter had tried to do some recruiting during the war - in Kerry, I think. She asked an old woman if none of her three sons were joining up. "Indeed no, my lady; it is much too dangerous." The girl said, "It is lucky that every one does not think like you." "It is indeed, my lady," was the answer to that.

All the more honour to those splendid Irishmen who did know the danger, and did not hesitate to go. Without doubt,

Major Redmond's death in action was one of the greatest misfortunes that ever happened to Ireland.

Discharged soldiers have a very different time in Ireland. There are numbers of them in Dublin, but very few venture to wear their service badges or medal ribbons.

Early one morning my husband was the only passenger inside a tram. He was in uniform, and the conductor, looking round to see that he was not observed, bent over him, and drew a Divisional Christmas card of the 5th Division in France out of his breast pocket, and whispered to him, "This is all I have now; they won't even let me wear my medal ribbons. I spent the twelve happiest years of my life in an Irish regiment. I am a Dublin man, but had I known what Ireland is like now, I would never have left the Army."

A few days before the November murders, I visited a military hospital near Dublin, where some scores of soldiers, wounded in the war, are still receiving treatment. I walked through the wards, talking to the men. Some of them had come from Lancashire, and had been sent to Dublin, as it was sufficiently near their homes. But I found several Irishmen. One of them was the type I had imagined all Irishmen to be like. I am glad I met this one.

He had been totally paralysed for three years, but had had some marvellous operation a few days before, and they hoped he might be able to walk a little in a few months' time. But when I saw him, he was still encased in plaster of Paris and bandages, and in fearful pain. I began to sympathise with him, but he looked up with a cheery grin, and said, "I ought to have better luck in the next war; I have had such bad luck in this."

Had he any opinions on the Irish question? I wonder. I could not ask him.

Among the people I pitied most in Dublin were the unfortunate professional men, who, in their endeavours to make a living, tried to steer a middle course between the two parties, and who generally ended in annoying both.

There was a cheery professor of dancing, a well-known figure in Dublin, who instructed all classes in the Fox-trot, Tango &c. One day a week he went to the Castle, where his pupils consisted entirely of officials and their wives.

We paraded solemnly up and down St Patrick's Hall, women at one end, men at the other. With set faces and harassed expressions, the Government of Ireland, Generals and Colonels, tried, with more or less success, to carry out the sharp commands of their stern instructor. The banners of the Knights of St Patrick, hanging on the walls, had surely through the ages never looked down on a more moving scene.

On other days, the same professor received pupils at his "Academy," by appointment. On four or five evenings a week, he arranged small subscription dances. His method of letting both sides know which of these dances they might safely attend was quite delightful. A notice was given out, somewhat as follows:

Dances will be held on three nights a week
Monday - Evening dress will be worn.
Wednesday - Evening dress will be optional.
Friday - Morning dress, and
on Friday evenings 'God save the King'
will not be played.

Was there ever a more tactful man? Of course, this was some months ago, and I do not imagine these dances are still being held.

CHAPTER III

My first dinner-party in Dublin

AFTER SECURING a flat, I had gone back to England to fetch my luggage, and, on my return journey, had my first experience of the Custom examination, which had just been started at Holyhead.

I was travelling with some friends, and between us we seemed to have at least half the luggage on the train. This was minutely examined for revolvers, ammunition, and bombs. A ham we had was a special object of suspicion. I had carried it most of the way. It was heavy, and it nearly made us miss the boat, for the Custom officials would prod it all over. They did not prod us, for which I was thankful, though I admit they should have done: it would have been so very easy to secrete several revolvers about one's person, to say nothing of ammunition.

There was no particular method of searching the luggage at Holyhead, and no counters or tables for the examination. I collected my luggage around me on the pier, as best I could, and felt like an agitated hen with a lot of chickens. Having got most of it together, one had to wait till some one came to examine it, and whether that was before or after the boat started was quite problematical. I dare say the arrangements are better now, but on my subsequent journeys to Ireland I was a privileged person, and was hurried on board the boat by my escort, who were all armed to the teeth.

I passed a dreary month of July in Dublin. It rained almost without pause. I believe it did the same everywhere else, but naturally I imagined beautiful summer weather all over England, and felt sure it was only wet and dismal in Ireland.

We had three consecutive fine days for the Dublin Horse Show. During the past twelve months I had attended horse shows in four different countries, but the Dublin Show was the best by a long way. The horses, the jumps, and the riding, especially of the women, were a revelation to me. They were, mostly, very badly turned out, but they could ride.

Horse Show week was the most peaceful one we spent in Ireland. There had been serious misgivings as to whether it would be possible to hold the show at all, owing to the disturbed state of the country. But the Sinn Fein leaders, when delicately approached on the subject, had guaranteed that there should be no disturbances of any sort. In fact, they even went so far as to say that a murder they had arranged for that week in Cork should be put off to the following week. When it is a question of money coming into the country, republicanism takes a second place.

We tried to play tennis, but the sodden courts never dried, the balls got black in a few minutes, and it was a dreary amusement. I had not been allowed to bring my dog from England to Ireland, owing to the quarantine regulations. I suppose it was right, though I really cannot see that, even if a few cases of rabies had occurred in Ireland, they would have been ever noticed among all the other excitements. By this time I was extremely bored because I did not have my horse in Ireland, and I had nothing of my own to ride.

An invitation to dinner from a General we had known on the Rhine, and who now occupied a high official post in Dublin, was quite an event.

A motor came to fetch us, which was lucky, as I am certain that no taxi would have driven up to his house. I wondered why there was another man sitting beside the driver and why he kept his hand in his right-hand coat pocket. I knew the reason for that, and for many other things, before I returned home that night.

The General then lived in an ordinary house on the outskirts of the town. He has since moved into safer quarters. In the room into which we were shown were one or two revolvers lying about, and at a noise on the landing one of the Staff turned sharply, and asked a servant, "What was that?" I smiled, and wondered why he was so nervous.

When we went into the dining-room I found a revolver laid beside each plate - knives, spoons, forks, and revolvers, in fact. The General who had taken me into dinner, said, conversationally, "This is just the sort of night they would come."

I said nothing, but looked around to see where, if "they" came, I could take cover. But the room was singularly bare, and even the tablecloth did not reach the floor. I nervously ate my oysters, and thought that, perhaps, on the whole, I after all preferred dining at home.

There were only two other ladies in the party: one, apparently, an enthusiastic Sinn Feiner. She started on my husband, without wasting a moment. He, having ascertained that she did not eat oysters, was quite happy to finish her share, as well as his own, and let her talk. Finding him so unresponsive, she turned to the General, and from then onwards I never got another word in; and we had been so

happy discussing racing on the Rhine, a much pleasanter subject than the I.R.A.

The lady soon got very excited, and the whole table had to listen. She was trying to convert us all, I think.

The General, who was always charming, listened politely but was obviously bored. She asked him to go round the country with her, to visit the people in the cabins: her poor, unhappy countrymen. "Richer, man for man, than any country in Europe," broke in a cold voice from the other end of the table. The same voice suggested to the General that perhaps it would be well to take a revolver in his hand before he toured the country. "And a tin of Keating's powder in the other," I added. [I had not been a month in Dublin without realising the necessity of never being without this insect-destroying powder.] I tried to introduce a more frivolous tone into the conversation, but the lady was so desperately in earnest, so

35

determined to make the most of her opportunities, that I gave it up.

In a pleading tone she begged the General to tell her if he did not love her country. It seemed an inopportune question to ask a man, surrounded by a perfect arsenal of revolvers, a man who goes in daily risk of losing his life at the hands of the same "beloved countrymen."

He merely grunted, so she turned to me with the same question. I was feeling rather cross. I wanted to talk about our year in peaceful Germany; nearly every one at the table had been there with the Army of Occupation, and had enjoyed it as much as I had. In fact, I wanted to talk about anything as long as it was not Ireland. I also felt frightened. I did not like the revolvers lying about. They had upset me; and when I am frightened I am always cross. It takes me that way. So I answered, "No; I simply hate it."

Tiresome woman, she would go on; and shortly, as I had expected, she started on Cromwell. I registered a vow that before I went out again in Dublin I would read up carefully what Cromwell had and had not done in Ireland. He lived two hundred and fifty years ago, it is true, but the deeds of no one else since seem to count at all with a certain class of Irishmen. We once had a house in Buckinghamshire, in the stables of which Cromwell was reputed to have stabled his horses. Very good stables they were too. That was the nearest I had ever got to Cromwell. He was also reputed to have laid waste the surrounding country. But they seem to have forgiven him there. Indeed, they have absolutely forgotten him. I quoted to the Sinn Fein lady the saying of a famous American: "Englishmen never remember history, Irishmen never forget it, and Americans never read it."

Upstairs, after dinner, I had another shock. The bridge-table was ready - quite ready - cards, markers, and a revolver at each corner.

The General told me that ever since the murder of poor Colonel Smythe, one of his best friends in the Club at Cork, he had always had a revolver ready. It was just the moment of time that it took Colonel Smythe to take his revolver out of his pocket that cost him his life.

Alas! we were not allowed to play bridge even; we were still talked about. In spite of my rudeness to her, our talkative dinner companion asked me to go and see her, and be introduced to some of her friends who shared her views. But I never went. Soon after the murders of 21st November I received a long letter of sympathy from her, but I did not answer it. Somehow, from a woman holding her views, it struck a false note, and I did not want her pity.

Among other things she told us that night, I heard that for the last twenty years every child in the south of Ireland was brought up to hate England. They learnt to read from books which asked this and similar questions: "Which country in the world do you hate most?" Answer: "England." These same books, by the way, are partly paid for by money supplied by the English tax payer.

This lady appeared to be bringing up her son in the same way, although her husband was in a British regiment. The pity of it!

The extraordinary thing was that later on, when Dublin was becoming still more dangerous, she telephoned almost daily to the Military for protection; she declared that she was in great danger, and must have a guard, which was finally given her. Her love for her countrymen did not seem to be equalled by her trust in them at that time.

We dashed back home at a terrific pace through the crowded streets. Everybody was hurrying to get home before curfew. We hurried because it was never safe for these particular motors to go slowly through Dublin. A fast-moving motor is harder to hit with a bomb than a slow one.

The others hurried to get in before 11 P.M. After that hour, if found in the streets, they would be taken off in a military lorry to spend the night at the nearest police station; or if they did not stop when challenged, they ran the risk of being fired at. Dublin citizens do not take many risks as a rule.

Our next dinner-party was at the residence - I cannot call it simply a house - of another and a still higher official. A car was not sent for us, and the taxi we ordered never turned up. Whether because I had stupidly told him where we were going I do not know, but I suspected that was the reason.

We managed to collect another taxi, and started off, already very late. A slight argument with the sentry at the gate made us later still. He evidently did not like our looks, and was unwilling to let us pass in our humble taxi. However, our hostess had guessed the reason for our delay: it was such a common occurrence in Ireland. She told me that she had the greatest difficulty in entertaining. So many civilians were frightened at being seen too often at her house. [Every motor that drives through certain gates in Dublin is watched, the number taken, and the occupants noted. Perhaps, naturally, the ordinary residents were not very anxious that it should be their motors, so noted.]

The evening passed without incident. I did not actually see any revolvers on this occasion, though a certain slight bulkiness in several pockets roused my suspicions. I knew where to look now.

It always amused me to see with what delicate care the butlers helped visitors on with their coats. There was none of that tugging and pulling down in which English butlers indulge. The butler in Ireland knows better. Automatic pistols go off so easily.

On our way home we were held up at the corner of Grafton-street. An Army raid was in progress, all traffic was stopped, and we had to wait with the rest till an officer came and investigated us. It was a strange scene, and an unpleasant one. Crowds of scowling, sullen-looking men and women, and just a handful of very youthful soldiers and one lorry. I felt it quite probable that one side or the other would shoot us. Not on purpose, of course. But it would not be much consolation to know it was only a mistake, and as we sat with half a dozen rifles levelled at our car, I felt distinctly anxious. There was always a chance of a shot in the back from the crowd too. Doubtless, a good many of them carried revolvers.

I decided I would not go out again in Dublin at night; and I never did, except in an armoured lorry on the night of 21st November,and that was the most alarming experience I ever had.

CHAPTER IV

MOTORING WITH REVOLVERS READY

SOME ONE asked me recently, when motoring at twenty-five miles an hour through an English lane, whether we were going too fast, and whether I was nervous.

I thought of some of my motor drives in Ireland, and smiled at the idea. There I only felt nervous when we were not going fast. Though, up to 21st November, one only looked on life as pleasantly exciting. I never had the slightest idea of the risks we ran, and that we were ever in any real danger never entered my head. It amused me to motor out to golf with men who sat with revolvers on their knees. I thought they were very careful of themselves, just as I thought that the army of officials who lived in Dublin Castle, and never went outside the gates, valued their lives very highly. I am not quite sure that I do not still think so, though perhaps they are right. We used to joke about these officials, and say they would have to stop in the Castle till they became entitled to their pensions, and then leave Ireland by aeroplane.

The first time I went to play tennis at Dublin Castle, a

lady walked round the court during the game, and laid a wreath on the grass. Three of the victims of the 1916 rebellion were buried behind the tennis courts, and there they still lie. I am not sure that some of those who now live in the Castle do not envy their peace and rest.

I often asked friends, who did not venture out at intervals, to play tennis or golf with me; but I must own I always had a slight feeling of relief when they refused. I was not exactly frightened, as I have said, and I did not realise the danger they were in, nor that their presence was a source of danger to me; but as things got worse in Dublin, as they rapidly did in the autumn of 1920, I felt that it was better for them not to be in the streets and in unguarded houses. Still I did feel that it was cowardly and unkind not to ask them sometimes.

The one person who I was perfectly convinced was safe, luckily for my peace of mind, was my husband. He was a regimental officer working in the North Dublin Union with the Lancashire Fusiliers, and had nothing whatever to do with politics, secret service, or police. We were always told that the regular soldiers were popular, and that the people fully realised, as was, and is now, an undoubted fact, that the British officer stood between them and ruin. For had it not been for the regimental officers, and the discipline they enforced, Dublin would have been burned long ago.

I cannot understand how men can go on, week after week, month after month, motoring, living, sleeping, always in danger, always with their hands on their revolvers. They all agree that it is much worse than France, the strain far greater.

There is no "behind the line" in Ireland. There is no relief from the atmosphere of murder and spying. At every street corner, there is a knot of men and youths, any of whom may throw a bomb or fire a shot at you, in the absolute certainty that, in that event, no one will give them away; and that they will be able to escape, with ease and certainty, down a side street or through a shop or house, leaving the innocent passers-by to bear the brunt of any shots that might be fired in reply.

Meanwhile, these people all stare into your motor as you pass. Once, when I was walking, a motor passed me, which I recognised, as did a man who was standing near me. He stepped out into the road, read the number carefully, and wrote it in a notebook. I could not help turning round and laughing at him, and telling him not to be so ridiculous. I have never seen any one so taken aback. The numbers on these motor-cars are always being changed, which must worry the Sinn Fein picquets a little; but there are hundreds of these men, who earn good pay by doing nothing but loaf about street corners, listening and spying. I suppose the new numbers are soon known. Of course, these Sinn Feiners have lists of people they want, and know them all by sight. These lists are often captured in raids, and it must be an odd feeling to see one's own name on the list to be removed as soon as possible.

An example of how unsettling such experiences can be concerns a little terrier running about Dublin Castle which no one will own. He is quite a happy little dog - every one is good to him, every one feeds him; but no one now will call him "my dog." His last three masters have all died violent deaths. The first died for his country fighting in France; the second and third were murdered in Ireland. That third master I knew rather well, and my husband very well. We were driving to a bridge tournament when we heard of his death. After five years of the war, I imagined I had no feelings left. I used to hear of horror after horror with dry eyes, and seemed to have become incapable of being moved very deeply by anything. But in Dublin these tragedies shook me to the depths. I hated to go out anywhere; I always seemed to hear some bad news, or get mixed up in some horrid disturbance.

For instance, one afternoon I was coming back with a friend by tram from a delightful day's golf, when I really had forgotten everything, and had begun to think that Ireland was not such a bad country after all. Just as we reached the middle of Dublin, our tram suddenly stopped.

I heard shots, and saw hundreds of people running madly in every direction. We got out of the tram and walked up a side street, where we found an outside car, and got on it. I asked the driver what had happened. A soldier, he said, had been killed, and the military had fired back and killed two civilians. In an unguarded moment - though I was generally very careful of what I said in public - I replied, "And a good thing too." He turned round in his seat with a look of fury, and said, "There are not many who would let you live to say that twice."

I could not get off the car, so I stayed on, feeling extremely uncomfortable, and feeling, also, that I hated golf and everything else, and that really one could not even attempt to make the best of things in a country where such incidents were possible, in fact common. I wondered what people would say in England if they were subject to those sorts of excitements and threats when coming home from a peaceful day's golf.

Sometime in September - about two months after I had arrived in Ireland - I was told by a Castle official, a man whose opinions should have carried great weight, that I had no right to be over there at all. Furthermore he declared that he strongly disapproved of officers' wives being in Ireland, and that he would not, on any account, have his own wife there, and that, if he had his own way, he would pack us all back to England at once. It was not safe for us, and, also, it hampered his work, as they were always afraid of reprisals on officers' wives.

There had been several rumours before this that we, the

wives, would have to leave Ireland. It was announced in one morning's paper, and contradicted in the next. But after being told this, as I considered, more or less officially, I felt sure that it must be only a matter of days before I should have to pack up and go.

But weeks passed, and nothing more was said. I asked once why we were allowed to stay, and was told that our leaving would make such a bad impression on Ireland. A curious reason for allowing us to remain; or, at least, I thought so later on. At the time I do not suppose that I thought about the matter at all. I was only too glad that I could be with my husband. I even had my little daughter over for a short time. While she was with us, the Sinn Feiners raided a house for arms a few doors from us. There was a good deal of firing, which I really thought for the moment was small boys playing with crackers. [The small boys of Dublin had a pleasing habit of exploding crackers to see us jump. I never disappointed them.]

I could not imagine real firing in our eminently respectable area, the Mayfair of Dublin, and although we leant out of the window to see what was happening, luckily it was too dark to see anything. [We heard later that two or three people had been slightly wounded.] My small daughter went to bed, much disappointed, and hoping that our house would be the next to be raided. Fortunately, when the time came - and it was very far from being a mere raid for arms - she was safe in England. I think I should have gone mad if she had been present on that ghastly day.

She and I used to ride together daily in Phoenix Park, but even there one could not get away from the war. Unfortunately, we never admitted we were at war though the Irish openly declared they considered they were fighting against England. Mysterious-looking men skulked about under the trees, watching everything and everybody, and numbers of R.I.C. and soldiers surrounded Viceregal Lodge and the Chief Secretary's residence. Later, when in more tragic circumstances, I myself stayed at the latter place, I was very glad the soldiers were there. No guard would have been too large to please me then.

On these visits to Phoenix Park, I always rode a mare that had been my husband's charge in France. Thanks to the kindness of the War Office, she had been sent over to him from Germany. I had ridden her there, and was rejoiced to see her again in Ireland. She had been wounded in the war, and always wore on her brow-band the three medal ribbons to which she was entitled. The soldiers loved this; not so the Sinn Feiners, and I got many unpleasant looks. I do not know how I could have been so stupid to ride her with those conspicuous ribbons, but one simply could not take things seriously, and the fact that it was an unsafe thing to do, and that I was asking for trouble never even entered my head.

If I did worry about anything - and I could not help thinking and worrying sometimes - I was always told that things were getting much better, and that the trouble would soon be over.

A few days before the November murders, a friend of mine, who had a flat in our house, was held up by two men outside the door at seven o'clock in the evening. They pressed a revolver against her chest, and asked her a number of questions, as to where she lived, and so on. Even this did not greatly alarm us. My husband did tell me that I must always be indoors before it was dark; and I made him promise that he would never walk to barracks alone in the evening. I suppose we must have got callous and indifferent, and every one was so heartily bored with it all, so tired of the place and the people.

Such things may have been boring to many of us, but for others these days and nights must have been terribly

45

exciting. I think that the two men who could really write a good book about Ireland in these times are Michael Collins, the Commander-in-Chief of the Republican Army, and Richard Mulcahy, his Chief of Staff. Amusing Irish stories are merely irritating at present, and, personally, I find it almost impossible to imagine that Ireland and the Irish people ever resembled the country and the characters portrayed in the delightful books I loved so much. Those same delicious characters are probably at this moment - if not actually engaged in murder at four hundred pounds per victim - digging trenches and mining roads for the small sum of seven shillings a day - this, I believe, being the tariff of pay in the Republican Army.

But Collins and Mulcahy's reminiscences would be wonderfully interesting and exciting. They might also be amusing, if they have a sense of humour. Practically every General, on every side, has written his own version of the great European war, so perhaps some day these two will give us a book on the Irish war.

One day in their lives, not to speak of the nights, must contain more incident than fifty years of most men's. The countless half-written letters and half-empty cups of tea that they leave behind them as they make their innumerable and hairbreadth escapes which, according to our people, they are perpetually making, sometimes over the roof, sometimes through the cellar, make a dramatic story. Sometimes Collins & Co. got away fully dressed, at other times they escaped in shirts and pyjamas. Their luck must turn some day, and they will be caught. Then perhaps they will write their book. But perhaps not: they may not have time to write it then. There can be no two opinions as to the courage and brains of these two at least. But what a life; what a waste of two really wonderful men!

I suppose, like us, they also motor with their revolvers

in their hands, for ever expecting that shout of "Hands up!" Words so familiar to both sides, but alas! from the Sinn Feiners it is usually followed quickly by a volley of shots.

"Hands up! What is your name?" The order is obeyed, the name given and, then, murder.

CHAPTER V

RAIDS

IN DUBLIN both officers and men rather welcomed a raid. It was a break in the monotony of the ever-lasting guards. There was always the hope of a scrap, of getting a little of their own back. When volunteers were called for, the whole regiment usually responded. Dressed in filthy old clothes and rubber-soled shoes, especially kept for what was frequently very dirty work, they sallied forth in parties of twenty or so, with one or more officers. These raids were usually done at night, and fearful secrecy was observed.

On these occasions, my husband would come back to our flat about tea-time as usual. He would stay for dinner, and then about 9 o'clock would suddenly announce that he was going out again, and that he would not be back that night. He was always so afraid that a chance word would arouse the suspicions of the Irish servants, who doubtless had their own means of communicating quickly with their friends outside.

No one who has not been in Ireland lately could possibly realise the marvellous organisation of the Sinn Feiners, and the enormous sums of money they have at their command for Intelligence work. Their information was wonderfully rapid and accurate, and they do not disdain the humblest instrument. The paper-boys, or the woman who sold flowers and who was allowed to sit in the hall of our building, were all part of their Intelligence system. Ever since 1916, when Asquith released the rebel leaders who were then in prison, they have been busy, while we were fighting for our lives, perfecting this system, collecting money, and organising the guerilla warfare which they are now waging so successfully. We did our best, by the strictest secrecy, to struggle against this marvellous information.

The officer in charge of these midnight raids would never even call for his volunteers until a few minutes before the raid was timed to start. In fact, he actually went round the barrack rooms and roused each man from his bed. [With all his many virtues, the British Tommy is a confiding person, and the ladies he met in the streets were often members of the I.R.A.] The party would then leave the barracks in a motor lorry, which went by a circuitous route towards the house which had been selected for the raid. Some few hundred yards away it would halt.

Leaving a few men to guard the lorry, the rest would run quickly and noiselessly towards the house, the plan of which had been carefully studied before leaving the barracks. Parties previously detailed went straight to the doors and various exits. When all were in position, a knock on the door with the butt-end of a rifle aroused the inhabitants.

After they had knocked, the two men at the door would spring immediately to one side, to avoid the very strong chance of a shot being fired through the panels from inside. Once the door was opened, the search party entered, leaving a strong picket outside. The occupants of the house usually presented a curious appearance in various odd deshabilles; they were generally terribly frightened, but when they realised the raiders were soldiers, and not the much feared Auxiliaries, they became calmer.

Beds, cupboards, chimneys were searched, and carpets raised. Ladies' clothing hanging in wardrobes was always carefully investigated. This was often a favourite hiding-place for revolvers, ammunition, or seditious documents. If the house was moderately clean this work was bearable, though unpleasant.

There is another side to this picture, and some of the descriptions given to me by officers, to whose unhappy lot had fallen the searching of some of the filthy tenement houses in which Dublin slums abound, made me quite ill.

A dozen people in a room, and five or six in a bed was quite usual; imagine searching such a bed and pulling the mattress to pieces. One officer told me that he had found four human beings, two ducks and a lamb, in one bed, not to speak of hundreds of smaller and unmentionable animals. A few days in hospital subsequent to a raid such as this, to get rid of a complaint common among the great unwashed, were often necessary.

It annoyed me so much that the men returning from a raiding party had always to submit to the indignity of being carefully searched. This was due to the whines and complaints, totally unjustifiable, of the Irish rebels, who invariably claimed compensation from the hated British Government for articles missing from their houses after a raid - articles which they had probably never possessed.

Even necessary damage, such as the breaking of a lock of a cupboard, or the accidental smashing of a pane of glass, was always paid for.

In one such early morning raid, ten officers and 120 other soldiers searched three houses in Drumcondra for a well-known Sinn Feiner. Afterwards, the owner of one of the houses had the effrontery to claim that savings of £17.10.0 had gone missing. The claim was totally without foundation. None the less, new guidelines on how soldiers should conduct themselves on these raids were issued in August. They stressed that the troops should adopt "a courteous but firm attitude towards the inhabitants of a raided house." Truly we are a nation of fools, even if gentlemen.

Of course, most of these night-time raids were only small and comparatively unimportant military exercises. The big daylight raids were often carried out by combined Auxiliary and military forces. It was quite a common occurrence, when going through Dublin, to find a whole street, or even a number of streets, closed. Tanks, lorries, armoured cars, all took part. No one was allowed to pass in or out of the street involved. Personally, I always retreated hurriedly, as did all sensible persons, when I found such a raid in progress. There was too much risk from a stray bullet, from either side, or a fragment of a Sinn Fein bomb.

These big raids were planned on an elaborate scale. Dozens of sentries picqueted every corner, a house-to-house search was made, and usually numerous arrests were effected. Throughout, tanks waddled slowly up and down the street.

The tank from our barracks usually hurried up a little late, and out of breath. This was due to the fact that as it left the barracks, it had to by-pass a civilian hospital and negotiate a narrow street, a hill and a nasty corner. The first time it came out it leant for a moment against the hospital's garden wall, which hastily collapsed like a pack of cards. Within half an hour a claim from the hospital authorities for compensation for wanton destruction was in the Colonel's hands, and, as usual, it was fully paid.

During these raids, ever the most awe-inspiring sight for me was the car-loads of Auxiliaries: eight or ten splendid-looking men, in a Crossley tender, armed to the teeth, and

flying a large black-and-tan flag. On the tan half a large "B" was painted; on the black bit, the letter "T". [I have the flag of the 169th Prussian Infantry that flew over Bonn Barracks before the arrival of our troops, also a Sinn Fein flag captured in a raid in Dublin. I should like to add to my collection one of these new Black and Tan flags - the colours of the only force that since the days of Cromwell has ever ruled Ireland.]

I know little of what the Auxiliaries have really done, or left undone, but I do know that they have put the fear of God into the Irish rebels. When criticising them, it should never be forgotten that these men are the survivors of the glorious company of those who fought and died for England. They themselves, at least, still remember their fallen comrades. For I saw them, a quiet little group, with uncovered heads, on Armistice Day, during the two minutes of what should have been silence. Only half a dozen other people near me in the crowded noisy street in which I stood paid any attention to the two minutes appointed for the remembrance of a world's sorrow, and somehow this attitude of callous indifference among the general public gave me more pain than anything else I saw in Ireland. The previous year, 1919, I was in Germany on Armistice Day. All the traffic was stopped. All heads bared, and conquerors and conquered alike united in tribute to their glorious dead: for the dead belong to no country.

There is, yet, a third sort of raid, which is undertaken by two or three daring spirits only. It occasionally happens that the whereabouts of some desperate and much-wanted member of the I.R.A. becomes known to the authorities. These rebels are always surrounded by their own particular body of guards and spies. The slightest attempt at an organised raid, on a large scale, would at once give the alarm, and the wanted men would quickly fade away, to appear shortly in another quarter of town. The only chance of getting them is a sudden dash. They are desperate men, and the raiders know well that shooting is bound to come, and it is just a question of who gets a shot in first. These raids usually end in tragedy.

I had absolutely no idea until after the November murders of the awful risks run by our men, when one of the few survivors of the original Intelligence Service opened my eyes to the dangers and difficulties of their lives. He would probably never have spoken then had not the horrors of that day shaken him to the depths. He told me of whole nights spent in lonely railway cuttings, when the slightest sound would have resulted in discovery and immediate death. Of long crawls over marshy fields, ending, perhaps, in a sudden dash and a volley of revolver shots. I had seen those men leaving the house, night after night, but I never knew or guessed what their work was, or still less, of the months of training they had had in this special work before going to Ireland.

Bloodhounds are sometimes used in raids [they have made many a fine photograph in the Irish newspapers], but are not very successful in Dublin. They quickly lose the scent in a crowded street, or the wanted man probably gets into a waiting motor-car, and escapes them that way.

Every old and new method is used to run the murder gang to ground, for until they are caught there can be no settlement in Ireland. But the majority of the population, if not actively helping the murderers, are at best passive. They are either terrorised or indifferent. History tells us that Ireland has always been indifferent to murder.

Finally, there was a fourth and unofficial form of raiding, but the time for that has passed now. Four or five of the older soldiers, who knew how to use their fists, would go into a public-house on the quays of the Liffey, and order drinks. Then, standing up, they would sing "God Save the King," insisting that every one else should stand up too. There are still Irishmen who love an open fight, and both sides enjoyed these comparatively bloodless battles. Alas! much blood, as well as water, has passed under O'Connell's Bridge since those days and both sides now, when they fight, fight to kill.

CHAPTER VI

TRAVELLING IN IRELAND

A VISIT to an Irish racecourse had for years been an ambition of my life. We arranged to go to a meeting at the Curragh. We were to lunch with some friends there first, and we were looking forward to it immensely. My husband took a day off, and, dressed in our best, we went down about nine o'clock to the waiting taxi. It was actually there, too.

The driver, however, when I told him to drive to Kingsbridge Station, was discouraging. "It is no use going there, the trains are off; you won't get to the races to-day." However, he did not give any reason, and thinking he was talking nonsense, we said we would go and see.

The station looked very much as usual. The train was waiting, and there were a few people sitting in the carriages, and a large crowd on the platform. I did not see any engine, but I did see a dozen men of the R.I.C. carrying their rifles.

I feared the worst, as I had heard that the railwaymen were refusing to carry armed police or soldiers. But I thought surely the Irish were too sporting to let just a few men spoil a race meeting, and we went to take the tickets. No good. The train would not start. The engine-driver would not bring back his engine until the R.I.C. went home. We asked the officer in charge of the party if he did not think he could take his men home; but he said it would be impossible, and that he would stay there all day if necessary. He did stay there all day.

We heard afterwards that the first train left the station about five o'clock in the afternoon. None the less, we extracted a little mild amusement from seeing a few cabs and cars drive up late, laden with luggage, in a wild hurry to catch the trains, which we knew were not going to start; and after waiting dismally about we left. I went home by tram, and my husband back to barracks.

I despatched a gloomy telegram to my friends at the Curragh. For once I did not care what I wrote or said, or who heard me. It was an expensive telegram, but it was a slight relief to my feelings.

This proved to be my only attempt to attend races in Ireland. I was too disgusted to try again. The next time I was asked to the Curragh, it was to play tennis. In spotless white serge I sat in the railway carriage, waiting for the train to move. It apparently was going to start this time, and I felt quite cheerful and hopeful. A horrid-looking old man approached me, and said, "Are you going to emigrate?" I put out an immaculate white shoe and silk-clad leg, and very nearly kicked him. Did I look like an Irish emigrant? I was quite speechless with wrath. My friends shrieked with laughter when I arrived at the Curragh and told them the story, but for once I could not see a joke against myself. [The I.R.A. were endeavouring to stop the emigration of all able-bodied men and women. They needed them all in their army, for the women are almost as useful as the men. So they watch the railway stations, and question all likely-looking people, and try to persuade them to return to their homes. Apparently, I was deemed a potential emigrant. What an awful thought!]

Our next journey by train was from Dublin to Belfast. We were going on ten days' leave to Scotland. We were very doubtful if we should get away, as the Lord Mayor of Cork, Terence MacSwiney, had been hunger-striking since August, and we knew that, if he died, it was probable that all leave would be stopped. But he had been dying for so long; every plan we had made for weeks was always made with the proviso that, if he died, the arrangements would be cancelled. So we determined to start at any rate, and to trust to luck and to the Lord Mayor not to be recalled.

Half-way between Dublin and Belfast the train stopped at a small station, and, to our disgust, about fifty armed R.I.C. boarded the train. There was a fierce and prolonged altercation, in which every one took part. We had allowed ourselves one hour and a half to get from one station to the other at Belfast. We were catching the boat from Larne to Stranraer, and motoring from Stranraer to our destination, where there was a big shoot the next morning.

With dismay, we saw the minutes slipping away, while the engine-driver argued as to whether he would, or would not, remove his engine. At last he decided to go on. We were very late by then, but when we did arrive at Belfast, more trouble awaited us. About a mile from the station I looked out of the window, and saw soldiers guarding the line with fixed bayonets, one soldier about every fifty yards. What could they want? We were in Ulster, Union Jacks waved from almost every building, and I really felt safe at last. In fact, what they wanted was some one on our train.

The station in Belfast was crowded with troops, and the porter said it was no good moving our luggage, as neither passenger nor luggage would be allowed to leave the train. Truly the woes of unfortunate people who travel by train in

Ireland are many. The boats to Scotland only leave every twenty-four hours, and twenty-four hours in Belfast out of only ten days' leave was not an inviting prospect.

But the soldiers were Scotch and the officer was kind. They accepted my husband's word that he was an officer on leave, and that I was his wife - the soldiers seemed to be looking for a particular woman. I implored them to let me go through. I said I was myself Scotch, that I was going to Scotland, and that I simply must get away from this hateful country. And they smiled, and let me pass.

So, walking through lines of bayonets, we eventually left the station, with about seven minutes to get across the city.

We did it at a gallop, with our luggage piled on to an outside car. I had rather hated those cars till then; but it is wonderful what they can carry, and what they can do. No one but an Irish jarvey would have galloped through those crowded slippery streets. One large trunk apparently rested on the horse's tail. The driver was perched on my hat-box, and we clung on at the back. Not that I ever did anything else but cling on an outside car. I never did acquire the art of lolling gracefully. We caught the train, and I sank into a seat, with my legs feeling like cotton wool. I did not really recover till I stood on Scotch soil, where I nearly hugged the porter, with his heavenly Scotch voice. It was good to be there again.

Almost as soon as we arrived in Scotland, the Lord Mayor of Cork died, but my husband, to our surprise, was not recalled. Other officers who were on leave from England had to return, because of the railway strikes; but, as we explained, a railway strike or so was nothing to us. They were not noticed among the other disorders in the country we came from.

During our ten days in Scotland, I was amazed at the interest taken in Ireland by the country people where we were staying. Even the old keeper who took me fishing had a great deal to say on the subject. He explained that it was not the murdering he minded so much, as the fact that no one lifted a hand to help the unfortunate victim; and he quoted the case of the poor man who was dragged out of a tram in a crowded Dublin street, without the slightest effort being made by any one to stop the murderer. That, he thought, was very cowardly. I agreed with him it was.

I found people in England at this time were very apathetic about Ireland; there was far more feeling in Scotland. There is no doubt that the religious question has got a good deal to do with it; Ulster and the West of Scotland are very near akin, and they detest the Roman Catholic Church. There is no doubt, also, that the sympathies of Roman Catholic countries are largely with the south of Ireland. Even in Belgium, which owes nothing to Ireland, and so much to England, there is a considerable group that actively supports the Sinn Fein cause, both with sympathy and with money. This can only be owing to the influence of the Church, which assists the vigorous Sinn Fein propaganda in that country and others.

A friend of ours in Brussels, a Belgian lady, took a photograph of my husband to be framed, shortly after the November murders. She explained to the woman in the shop that he had been nearly killed in Dublin in the massacre of the previous Sunday. The woman replied, "I am sorry if he was a friend of yours, but what a splendid thing it was." To me, if I did not know it to be true, this remark would be absolutely unbelievable. I was in Brussels with my husband just after the Armistice, and I shall never forget the enthusiasm of the people for every British soldier. When we got into a tram, every one got up to give us seats, and everybody said something nice about the English General. Two years later, when that same officer is the victim, with many other British officers, of a brutal attack, a Brussels shop-keeper says, "How splendid!"

We finally got back to Ireland without incident on 3rd November. I believe in presentiments, and in no other way can I account for the horrible feeling of depression I felt during the next weeks. Naturally I did not like going back, but it was more than that. I felt absolutely and utterly miserable. I missed one officer who had a flat in the house, and was told that he had gone on leave. Later on, when I went to see my husband in hospital, I found that, far from being on leave, he had been badly wounded in a raid while we were away. I must own that, at this time, I did feel rather nervous occasionally. There were four Secret Service men living in the house, and two others came in to meals, and I did wonder sometimes if it was safe for them and for us. By this time, my husband very frequently slept in barracks. Now nearly every night there was firing, usually just a shot or two, but sometimes a regular volley.

The whole atmosphere of the place was more than ever hostile, and I struggled with my depression, and told myself it was only because I had been so thoroughly spoiled in Scotland. But it was no good. Even the servants in the house seemed different; certainly one of them did. I thought, too, that I was followed home once or twice, and could not understand why such an unimportant person as myself should be watched. But I realise now that they watched every one who went to and from that ill-fated house in Dublin.

CHAPTER VII

RED SUNDAY

EXTRACT from *The Times*, Monday, 22nd November: -

"At nine o'clock yesterday morning gangs of assassins
visited simultaneously a number of selected houses and
hotels in Dublin, and in circumstances of revolting
brutality murdered at least fourteen British officers and
ex-officers, and wounded five more. In two or three cases
officers' wives were pulled out of bed, and their husbands
murdered before their eyes."

Extract from a letter written by Father Dominic, a
Roman Catholic priest, who was arrested a few weeks later: -

"Sunday, November 21st, was a wonderful day in Dublin."

Above are two points of view, English and Sinn Fein, of
one of the most ghastly massacres the world has ever known.
It is exactly three months to-day since "Red Sunday" in

Dublin. I am writing this on a Sunday morning, again in Dublin; like 21st November, it is a fine sunny day. In the distance I hear the sound of church bells. They were ringing that Sunday morning too, summoning the people, some to Mass, and others to murder.

My husband had hurried over his dressing, as he was to take a Church Parade at the Commander-in-Chief's. I was wearing a blouse with a lot of tiresome little buttons. Had it not been for those silly little buttons I should have gone down to breakfast with my husband, and should have had the agony of seeing him and others killed or wounded before my eyes, and should probably have been shot myself.

I was standing at my bedroom window struggling with the cuff of my blouse, when I saw a man get over the garden wall, which was about 10 ft. high and covered with ivy. I watched him idly; in spite of five months in Dublin and constant alarms and excitements I felt no fear, and not much anxiety. I thought he had come to see one of the maids. But directly I saw him take a revolver out of his pocket my fears were aroused, and I rushed to the door, and shouted to my husband, who had left the room a few minutes before.

It is a bitter thought now that if I had raised the alarm directly I saw the man get over the wall I might have roused some of the other officers, though I believe from the evidence collected that it is fairly clear that several of the murderers were already in the house when this man got into the garden. Their organisation was perfect.

My husband was unarmed. The staff and regimental officers who occupied flats in this and, I believe, other similar buildings, had been warned and advised that it would be wiser not to carry revolvers or to keep them in their rooms: on the same principle, I suppose, as the Dublin Metropolitan Police were also unarmed - *i.e.*, if you did not hurt any one, no one would hurt you, and if we had no weapons in our rooms we should not be raided, and Sinn Fein raids had been frequent in our neighbourhood. Accurate information as to where such weapons would be found was apparently always given by servants in the various houses.

The other officers who had rooms in the house each, I know now, had several revolvers, but they never used them. Not one of them fired a shot. I imagine they were surprised and shot down before they even had time to arm themselves.

Our first thought was for those friends, Lieutenant-Colonel Montgomery of the Royal Marines and Captain Keenlyside of our own regiment, who lived on the lower floors and, after looking at the man in the garden, my husband rushed down to warn them, and to bolt the hall door.

It was too late. The hall was full of armed men, dressed in overcoats and rain coats and wearing cloth caps and felt hats. My husband was ordered to put his hands up and to give his name. He did so, and added, "There are women in the house." The murderers answered, "We know it." At that moment the door behind my husband opened, and he, fearing that one of the officers he had hoped to warn was coming out of his room, shouted, "Look out, Montgomery." As he spoke they fired and shot my husband through the shoulder, and he fell at the foot of the stairs. He scrambled up, but was shot again through the back. Getting up again, he half-walked and half-crawled upstairs.

Lieutenant-Colonel Montgomery, who had not heard my husband's warning, was also fired at twice, and fell at his wife's feet, she herself being grazed on the knee by a bullet. Montgomery died sometime afterwards.

I had remained in my room, watching from the window the man in the garden, who stood a few feet from the back entrance, revolver in hand, ready to fire if any one tried to escape through that door.

I heard six shots only, though subsequently I found at least fifty must have been fired; but the building, being two houses joined into one, was a large one, and except for these six shots the rest of the shooting took place on the other side of the house and on the other stairs.

I was in an agony of anxiety, but I had sworn to my husband that I would not leave my window. The door opened, and he came in. His shoulder was covered with blood, but his first words were, "It's all right, darling, they have only hit outlying portions of me. Go back to the window."

He looked much as usual, and as he had apparently walked upstairs [I can never understand how he got back to the room alone and unaided], I did not think he could be very badly hurt, so I did as I was told. Now I saw about twenty men running and cycling away down a lane, and I also saw the man in the garden being helped to escape by one of the servants from the flat, who came out with a key and let him out through a garage door. It was a dreadful moment. I had watched him so carefully, and I did think that he, at least, would be caught.

I then turned to my husband, and found to my horror that he was just losing consciousness, and that the bed on which he was lying was soaked with blood. I took off his coat, and saw four bullet holes - two in his arm and shoulder, a horrible-looking one in his back, and another in front. We found afterwards that these were two entry and two exit holes, but I thought at the time that he had received four wounds.

Never to my dying day shall I forget the scene in the hall and on the stairs, where four officers had been shot. There were great splashes of blood on the walls, floor, and stairs, bits of plaster were lying about, and on the walls were the marks of innumberable bullets.

Fortunately, the murderers had been so panic-stricken themselves and their hands so shaky that their firing had been wild in the extreme, and to this fact my husband and Captain Keenlyside, who was shot in the jaw and both arms, owed their lives.

I turned round the corner of the hall, and saw a patch of blue, and found a man in bright-blue pyjamas lying on the floor. He, I knew, had a flat on the fourth floor. Why they brought him down and shot him in the hall I do not know. I leant over him. He was shot through both lungs. I could do nothing, and I knew if I was going to help my husband I must think only of him, for there was a limit to my physical and mental powers of endurance. So reluctantly I left him.

The outer hall was by then full of people, and I found that doctors [one lived in 31 Upper Pembroke-street and a further five lived within a few hundred yards] had already been sent for. I then heard that two officers were lying dead upstairs, and the others in the hallway were dangerously wounded.

The dead were Major Dowling of the Grenadier Guards and Captain Price, formerly of the Middlesex Regiment. Both were fully dressed in their uniforms and were about to go downstairs for breakfast. Lieutenant-Colonel Montgomery, who was wounded in the hallway shootings, died afterwards. In fact, not one of the six officers who lived in the house had escaped in the attack.

I cannot describe the awful feeling of sick horror that came over me, and how I literally shook with mingled feelings of pity and passionate anger. I went to the telephone, rang up the barracks, and implored them to send soldiers at once, and then tore upstairs again to my husband.

I seized rugs and hot-water bottles from the bed of an old Irish lady who had the flat below us. I found her in a terrible state of agitation, cursing the British Government, but I had no time to waste on her.

At last the doctors came to my room. They told me they had already seen the other wounded, and, leaving them with my husband, I went downstairs again.

I expected the troops any moment, and I wanted to make sure that the servant I had seen helping one of the murderers to escape was arrested the moment they arrived. I could not rest till I knew the house was surrounded by soldiers. I feared the murderers might come back to finish their bloody task.

At last a party of our regiment arrived, and with them our soldier servant. This was the same man who had deserted the day after I arrived in Dublin. [He had not gone far before he repented and returned, and after he had served a term of imprisonment I had pleaded for him, and had been allowed to have him back as our orderly.] Thank God I had him with me that day. He was the one person in the house who remained unmoved and imperturbable. He had come to clean boots, but it was all one to him, and he did everything for everybody.

After an agonising period of uncertainty, the doctors told me they did not consider my husband's wounds dangerous, and shortly afterwards he was moved to the Military Hospital. The other more dangerous cases, including our own Captain Keenlyside, who was still in his pyjamas, were taken to a nursing home almost next door; but I was firm, and implored to be allowed to take my husband to our hospital. I would not have trusted any one I loved in any nursing home in Ireland that day.

It was arranged that I should move my things to the

barracks, so after taking my husband to the hospital, where the very sight of the matron and sisters inspired me with confidence, I returned to the Pembroke-street flat to lock up. The place filled me with loathing.

I found my orderly waiting for me with tea. I must have drunk buckets of tea that day - every few minutes some one brought me tea or brandy, or both, and I obediently drank it all. He had already tidied up my room and washed the hall and stairs. I found my husband's clothing soaking in the bath, and I could not help smiling, though I never felt less like smiling in my life, when we had a heated altercation as to whether Lux soap or salt was best for taking out blood-stains. I suggested Lux. He preferred salt.

Our regiment was still guarding the house when I returned, and some of the men came up and spoke to me. Several of them had tears in their eyes. They had heard my husband was dead. Many of them had served with him in Malta and India. Others had fought under him at the Dardanelles and along the duckboards of Ypres.

I wonder what those men thought when stretcher after stretcher was carried out in front of them, and they had not been able to fire a shot or strike a blow.

I think it speaks well for the magnificent discipline of our regiment that in spite of the fierce anger they felt, not one act of reprisal in any shape or form was taken by them that night or during the ensuing week. Later on a special order of appreciation and thanks was issued by the Commander-in-Chief.

I cannot end this chapter and this most horrible episode of my life without alluding to the courage and presence of mind of the wives of the murdered officers.

Our house was only one of the many that was visited that morning. Even more ghastly scenes were enacted than those I have tried to describe.

Everywhere it was the same story of ruthless murder, and of bravery and self-control on the part of the women. It had been much easier for me than for any of the others, as I did not actually see any of the shooting; I only saw the aftermath.

In one house there was a friend of mine whose husband from the first was seen to be dying, and she had been wounded too by a bullet, meant, I suppose, for him as he lay in her arms. Another friend had been pulled out of bed with her husband, and had seen him led away to be shot. She was in the state of health when no woman could be expected to have much control over her nerves.

Another wife had gone from one dying man to another, for, as she said, she could not bear to think that either of them might recover consciousness before the end and find himself alone.

But except for the hysterical shrieks of one or two of the maids, I never heard a cry or saw signs of fear. Every one was perfectly quiet and self-controlled. Two or three of the Irish newspapers, as well as several English ones, said that the one bright spot on that awful morning was the bravery of the wives, [in the *Daily Mail* we were referred to as the "Brave British Women in Dublin who had proved themselves once again a race of heroines"] and they were right.

CHAPTER VIII

THE FOLLOWING DAYS

IT WAS not until I went back to the military hospital on the afternoon of 21st November that I realised that our house had not been the only one visited by the murderers. [In fact, in nearby Lower Mount-street, a running gun battle had taken place when the raiders were surprised by a number of Auxiliary police who were passing by and one of the murder gang was taken prisoner.] The hospital matron told me that the dead bodies of fourteen officers, many of them born in Ireland, lay in the hospital mortuary. Nine of these were in pyjamas. That little sentence shows in what circumstances the majority of them lost their lives.

Among the dead were two officers who had dined at our house on the Saturday night. These men were Roman Catholics, and, I was told, had taken up special service work from a sense of duty.

Tale after tale of horror was unfolded to me until my brain reeled, and I felt I could bear no more. One officer had been butchered in front of his wife. They took some time to kill him. [Shortly afterwards she had a little baby. It was born dead, and a few days after she also died.]

The American Consul had dined at the Pembroke-street house the night before the murders. His two hosts were among the murdered. They had played bridge till it was very late, and he had been pressed to stay the night. If he had, there would probably have been an American citizen the less, as there is no doubt the men and boys who visited our house were mostly quite incapable, from fright, of distinguishing friend from foe.

Captain Keenlyside of our own regiment told me he had been placed against a wall in the hall, and a group of men took, or tried to take, careful aim at him. One man's hand shook so much that a comrade took his revolver away from him, and another supported his trembling right hand on his left arm. Like my husband, this man also was a regimental officer, and had nothing to do with police or secret service. He too had a most marvellous escape, and none of the shots he received were vital.

Although my husband had been wounded twice during the Great War, the events in Dublin naturally had a more immediate effect on me. But when I left the hospital that afternoon, I felt fairly happy about him. He was very anxious that I should leave for England the next day, but I refused to leave him till the end of the week, and it was arranged that I should occupy his room in the barracks, which were near the hospital. When I got there, I found another officer's wife had also arrived to take refuge. Her husband had been very badly wounded, and had been taken to a nursing home near Pembroke-street.

She had been told that she could see him again at eight o'clock that night, and asked me to go with her. We ordered a taxi, not realising yet the gravity of the situation. Shortly before eight we heard that no motors of any description were allowed on the streets. The trams were stopped. During the afternoon there had been a fight between the Crown forces and Sinn Feiners in the Croke Park football field. This, added to the morning's murders, had inflamed both sides in Dublin to a dangerous degree. My friend said she would walk. It was nearly three miles through the nastiest parts of Dublin, and though not realising that this was quite impossible that night, I did not like the idea.

Fortunately an armoured lorry was going out on duty. The patrol had orders to stop and search all motors, and it was arranged that we should go with it. We sat in front of the lorry with the driver, and an officer and a party of soldiers behind. I did not see any armour, and felt singularly conspicuous and unsafe.

Never, if I live to be a hundred, shall I forget the Dublin streets that night. They were crowded, though one would have thought only fools would have been out at such a time.

There was firing everywhere, and occasionally the crash of a bomb. We dashed along at a terrific pace. The driver was longing to run over some one. The men were longing to shoot. They were mad with passion. One motor-car did not stop when challenged, and they fired at once. Fortunately they missed it. It was an R.I.C. car, going from one hotel to another, collecting luggage belonging to the survivors of the morning's massacre, who had already been moved into the Castle and other safer places.

When we arrived at the nursing home, the scene was a strange one. There was a military guard, inside and out. Three officers were lying there, dangerously wounded, and it was thought possible that the Sinn Feiners might come back to finish them off. In spite of all I had seen and heard that day, I could not think this was possible. [But since then a former soldier, who had been badly wounded, was carried out of a hospital on a stretcher and shot in the garden, so I suppose it really was possible, even likely.] The house was dark and quiet, the usual smell of anaesthetics pervaded the place, and in the dim light I saw British soldiers with steel helmets and fixed bayonets standing on the landings in the hall, on the stairs, and before each door.

My friend's husband was slightly better, and I persuaded her to return to barracks with me. The drive was equally exciting, rather more so. The gun fire was nearer to us now and we passed several Crossley cars full of Black and Tans. Our armoured lorry made a terrific noise on the paved roads, and as we passed, people fell on their knees on the pavements. Nearly every one had their hands up, and ran distractedly about. I could feel no pity for them. I hated them. I know nothing about reprisals. I believe nothing in Ireland that I do not actually see myself; but I do know that night I should have understood, and forgiven, any act of reprisal by our men. But, as I have already said, no act of reprisal took place.

I do not think I slept more than a couple of hours each night all that week. I never felt tired, never wanted to rest. On Monday - the day new, tighter, curfew regulations came into force - telegrams and telephone messages from England began to pour in. I had been so used to the apathetic attitude of English people, including my own friends and relations, towards Irish affairs, that I was overcome by the flood of messages of sympathy and offers of help that I received.

I did not realise how fully the awful affair had been reported in the English papers. England seemed awake at last.

I walked about freely on Monday, but on Tuesday I took an outside car, and went back to our flat to finally pack up our belongings. To my astonishment the car-driver knew who I was; and I was still more astonished when he asked me how my husband was getting on, and whether he would be likely to know any of the men who had shot him. As a matter of fact he would not; it was all over too quickly. Then came a string of leading questions. I looked at the man. He was the usual type of Sinn Feiner. He must have thought me a fool. However, I answered pleasantly and evasively - I might even say untruthfully.

When I got to the flat, I found various odd-looking people had been to ask for me, and had retired discomfited when they heard I was in the barracks. I did not like all this very much, and I packed, looking nervously over my shoulder all the time. Fortunately my faithful soldier servant arrived. He packed perfectly, as he did everything else. Was there ever any one like the British soldier? He looked after me all that week like a nurse. There was always a huge fire in my room when I got back from hospital. My fire lighted and my early morning tea brought to me at seven o'clock; my hot bath, and my breakfast in my room a little later. But, for all the care and kindness I had from every one, it was a ghastly week. I was interviewed by innumberable officials and journalists. I signed papers and made statements, and on Tuesday some of the relations of the poor murdered men arrived. I saw them, of course, but I could tell them so little, so painfully little.

The papers I filled in were really rather amusing. Among the questions to be answered were, "How many murders were committed in your presence?" &c., and next, "Were the murderers armed?" I felt inclined to answer this last like the wounded British Tommy, "No, they bit."

On Tuesday night, G.H.Q. suddenly got agitated about me, and all sorts of messages arrived to say that I was not to leave barracks without an armed escort. Apparently they wanted me later as a witness, so I became suddenly quite precious.

My husband was going on splendidly, so I arranged to

cross to England on the Friday. My husband, and the officers in whose charge I was, were most anxious that I should go sooner. On the other hand, the police authorities, who wanted my evidence, were equally anxious that I should not go at all. But I promised faithfully to come back, and I was allowed to depart.

I felt that I must really go away for a little, or I should go mad. It was horrible, feeling that the loafers at the street corners might now be watching and waiting for me.

Incidents I had laughed at before now became very real to me. I had gone through a great deal, and I could not rest in Ireland. I wanted to go to England; I wanted to feel safe. Above all, I wanted to get away from the sight and sound of revolvers.

All night too, there were sounds of rifle-shots, and the rattle of armoured cars returning to barracks from raids and patrols. These drew up, and the officer in charge made his report just below my window, which was not conducive to slumber.

Occasionally a sentry got nervous, and let off his rifle at a real or imaginary shadow in the garden of the female lunatic asylum opposite. This garden had been used as cover for Sinn Fein snipers, and my building in the barracks had been hit more than once. The other charming view from my window was over the ground of the pauper hospital. I really do not know which was the most cheerful outlook.

I motored to the Military Hospital two or three times, escorted by Auxiliaries. It gave me confidence just to look at them. They were so big, and so very fully armed. They also took me to the boat when I at last left Dublin. An officer and my faithful soldier servant went with me to my destination in England.

It was a long way away, deep in the English countryside, and it seemed like heaven. As my motor drew up to this secluded country house, the hall door opened, and I saw the big square hall and a huge log fire. My eyes filled with tears. Ireland seemed like an evil dream.

CHAPTER IX

RETURN TO DUBLIN

AFTER I had been in England a few days, I began to feel as if I had imagined the whole of the events of the last awful week. Surely such things could not have happened in the twentieth century in what we supposed was a civilised country. It was utterly impossible.

Night after night I went over the whole of that ghastly day in my sleep. Every night I woke up to see a ghoulish figure creeping up the garden path with a revolver in his hand. I heard the shots, and saw the blood-stained hall and stairs, and the figures of the dead and dying. I saw my friend in her pink nightgown covered with her husband's blood. I saw my husband lying wounded on the bed. And I shall see it as long as I live. I dreaded the thought of going back to the accursed country; for every stick and stone of it will be for ever hateful to me.

I had been in England about a fortnight, when I received a letter from the Authorities, saying that my presence would be required at a trial in Dublin that week. The trial concerned the murder of Lieutenant-Colonel Montgomery, the officer my husband had tried in vain to warn on that fateful day in November. I was informed that I ought to be ready to start at once on the receipt of a telegram, probably the following day, as the trial would be early in the week. The letter went on to say that I should be accommodated in a hotel in Dublin, which had been taken over by the Government for witnesses, and that I should be well guarded. By now martial law had been declared in many parts of the country and any trial that would take place would be a field general court-martial - conducted through the office of the Judge Advocate General. [Such a field, or overseas, general court-martial was smaller and simpler to convene than the more cumbersome general court-martial.]

I wired back to say that I would go, but added that I was staying in a house five miles from a station, and the motor could not go out because of the deep snow on the roads, and would they give me twenty-four hours' notice if possible?

I also wrote and said that I would do all I possibly could to help them, but I utterly refused to stay at any hotel in Dublin. I had friends in the Castle and Royal Hospital, who I knew would put me up, and where I should feel a great deal safer than in a hotel. Besides which, I had stayed at the best hotel in Dublin, and I trembled to think what the worst would be like, and I did not think it likely that the Government would run to even the second best. I prepaid the reply to my telegram.

All that day and the next I waited as patiently as I could for an answer. None came. I could not endure the waiting, so I wired again. Still no reply. Then I wrote, but that was no good. From the first I had volunteered to go back. I thought my evidence might be useful, and I was willing to go. I felt it was all I could do for the poor murdered men. I do not very often want to do disagreeable things: I generally spend my life in evading them. But this time I did want to do what I thought was right. The desire rapidly abated, as I waited day after day and week after week, without even an acknowledgement of my letters or wires.

By now my husband had arrived from hospital, and he started to write. At last he received a vague letter to say the trials had been postponed, but they expected they would be held shortly. Why they had not had the courtesy to let me know this at once I do not know. Meanwhile I heard privately from Dublin that the man for whose trial I was going over had been released from prison, so I began to hope that I should not be required. Vain hope.

We had gone to stay with some friends in the country, and were walking in the garden, when their intensely correct and pompous butler came out, and said in a most disapproving voice to my husband, "You are wanted by the Police, sir." This proved to be a message from Scotland Yard through the local police, to say that the trial would be held after all, and would we go over as soon as convenient?

Arrangements had been made for us to stay at the Chief Secretary's Lodge in Phoenix Park, and an escort would meet us at Kingstown, if we would kindly wire the date of our arrival. A letter confirming this arrived the same night. Apparently they had rearrested the prisoner, and decided to try him after all. Just a little touch of Irish humour, but rather hard on the prisoner and on me. By this time I had lost all wish to go. I was frightened of Ireland, and I only wanted to try and forget.

However, we started, and I was comforted by the thought that at least I should be safe and comfortable in the Chief Secretary's Lodge. But I had forgotten the curious habits of Irish officials in Ireland, and that a letter or two is nothing to them.

We arrived at Kingstown at the usual hour of 6 A.M. Other

people were met by motors - the King's Messenger and several other officers drove off. We scorned all offers of help. Were we not important witnesses? Were we not going to stay at an official residence?

Every moment I expected a large car and the promised escort to arrive. My apprehension was underscored by recent Army Intelligence reports that the practice of Sinn Fein rebels dressing in British uniforms was still very much alive and that second-hand clothes shops were reported to be doing a brisk trade in officers' and soldiers' uniforms.

We waited over an hour. It was quite dark and very cold. At last we crawled into an open Ford car that had come to meet two policemen from Liverpool. They, being wise men, had apparently not arrived.

We were tired, hungry, and very cross. About a mile out of Kingstown we met a motor, which stopped when they saw us. It was the promised car, escort and all, one hour and a half late.

An officer handed us a letter. I tore it open. It simply said that the arrangements for accommodating us at the Chief Secretary's Lodge had fallen through, and that rooms had been taken for us at a hotel on the Quays. The writer hoped we might be "reasonably comfortable," and added, the hotel was well guarded, and there were sentries on the roof.

I had often passed that hotel, and knew it well, for what it was, a pot-house - twenty sentries on the roof of that morally deficient establishment would not make it any cleaner.

My temper used to be fairly good, but Ireland had ruined it. I do not like to think now what that escort must have thought of me. I decided at first to return to Kingstown, and to take the same boat back to England, but I felt there was such a lot of things I wanted to say first to several people in Dublin Castle. So we drove in gloomy silence to the Castle.

It was about eight o'clock by now, but the Castle

inhabitants are not early risers. Poor things, they work most of the night. Ordinarily, I only feel pity and admiration for most of them, but that morning it added insult to injury to find no one up. No fire anywhere, no food, no one to swear at. I lighted a fire with my evidence for the court-martial, which I had written out so neatly.

Eventually sleepy orderlies arrived, and I took refuge in the house of a General, who was a friend of ours. We had several friends, too, on his staff. They were very sympathetic, and quite horrified at the way I was treated.

After a bath and breakfast I felt warmer and happier. One or two police officials came to see me, but I refused to be soothed. To one I said, "Who was the idiot responsible for there being no motor to meet us?" To which he replied nervously, "I was. As a matter of fact I looked up the boat in an old time-table. It used to arrive at eight o'clock, so I ordered the motor for that hour." This was too much for me, and I had to laugh. This was Ireland at its brightest and best.

I was persuaded to stay and give my evidence, but the problem as to where we were to stay had not yet been solved. Every one, without exception, agreed the suggested hotel was quite out of the question for any woman. By this time I was too tired and bored to care much where I went. Some one eventually wired to the Chief Secretary, who was in London, to ask if he really had withdrawn his previous offer of his house. In an hour back came his answer. Of course we were to go there; we were expected. So it was "only" some one's mistake. A very unpleasant mistake for me.

We drove to Phoenix Park just as it was getting dusk. The streets seemed fuller than ever. The usual groups of men at all the corners stared into the car as we passed. They looked even more sullen, more menacing, than formerly. Oh, it was horrible to be back again!

A cheerful black cat met us in the hall of the Chief

Secretary's Lodge. It was a particularly vulgar-looking animal. There were at least four others like it, each more common that the last. But they were all so nice and friendly, so very pleased to see me. It was a good deal more than any one else had been that day. I loved them for it, and did my best to reward them at meal-times.

The next day I found, to my dismay, that we were only wanted this time for the summary of evidence, and that I should have to go over again to Ireland in about three weeks' time for the court-martial itself. In Ireland, of course, if they said three weeks, it probably meant six, and I felt that I should never be finished with this detestable business.

I was also told that the police authorities would be very grateful if I could identify one of the murderers among the men who had been arrested since 21st November.

I gave my evidence at the summary, in front of the prisoner. There were only five or six people in the room, but I felt nervous, and my heart thumped. What would the court-martial itself be like!

Going round the prisons the day after was another unforgettable episode. We started off as usual in a closed car, at a great pace, followed by more cars full of detectives, every man with his hand in his right-hand pocket. I realised now very well what that meant. I sat buried in a fur coat, another fur up to my eyes. I did not like it a bit.

On arrival at the first prison an officer came out and took me up a sort of passage, telling me to keep very close to one side, as the other side could be seen from the top windows of the prison. I simply flattened myself against the wall. I was put into a little hut. The windows were covered with felt, into which slits about eighteen inches long and three inches high had been cut. It was explained to me that I was to stand with my eyes at one of these slits, and the prisoners would be paraded in front of me in batches of ten. They would be

numbered, and if I thought I recognised one of them I was to give the number to the officer at my side. I was also told that there was no cause for alarm, as the prisoners could only see my eyes, and could not possibly know me again.

There were about twenty other people in the hut - soldiers, detectives, one or two other women, and a little boy, whose father had been murdered before his eyes, and who had said "he thought he could recognise the man who killed daddy."

I felt almost too sick to look at the first batch of prisoners who arrived. Never have I seen such an unpleasant sight. They all seemed absolutely terror-stricken; they were shaking and gibbering with fright. They were not there to be shot, they were only there to be looked at, and yet they looked, I imagine, as a coward would look when facing a firing party. One or two nervously sucked cigarettes. I do not know why they were allowed to smoke at all. As each batch went away unrecognised by any one, some of them sang in a quavering voice a sort of song of triumph - or possibly relief. This noise was stupid and irritating.

It was the most extraordinary feeling to meet all those pairs of eyes. The prisoners had to look straight in front of them at the hut, and they stood there, licking their pallid lips, with quivering faces and shaking hands. They presented a sight not easily to be forgotten, and which, I hope, not many other women will have to see. Surely they must have been guilty of some crime, or they could not have looked as they did.

No one identified any one, and the procession of cars moved on to another prison. Here there was the same sort of hut, and again I stood with my eyes glued to a slit in the wall. I think I nearly fainted once. The atmosphere of the hut was very close, and I could not bear to look at all those men. I saw about two hundred altogether, and the strain was terrible. I know that some of them must have the blood of my friends on their hands. Some of them looked capable of any crime. But, unlike the first prison, where I had seen only the scum of Dublin, I saw a few fine-looking men here. One in particular had a wonderful face. He looked straight at the hut, and at the same time through it and beyond it. He stood with his head up, without a trace of fear. It was the face of a visionary. I wondered what crime he had committed, why he was there. Whatever he had done he was not ashamed of it. But then, alas! no Sinn Feiner is ashamed of murder.

Again I recognised no one, but one prisoner was identified by a man in the hut. It must have been a nasty moment for him when his number and name were taken and he was led away.

At last the long ordeal came to an end. So exhausted that I could hardly stand, I was conducted out of the prison, and we motored rapidly home, followed by some eight or nine detectives in Ford cars. The worst of it was that the Sinn Feiners were also nearly always clean-shaven men, and also went about in Fords, and I never knew whether I was being guarded or hunted.

I left for England that night. How I wished I had not got to return. Every one promised, from the Commander-in-Chief downwards, to get the court-martial through as soon as possible. I knew there would be no rest or peace for me while it was hanging over my head, a shadow on my life.

The journey back was much more successfully arranged. They seemed anxious to make amends for our arrival - the arrangements for which had certainly not inspired me with confidence. Perhaps it would be wiser not to mention all the precautions that were taken. I never know whether to laugh or to cry, some of them were so very funny. The name selected for me to travel under was so original; the Intelligence Officer who had thought of it was so obviously proud of his choice, and I tried hard to remember to answer when addressed by it.

But it was too much for my gravity when the procession of armoured cars, &c., pulled up at Kingstown pier, and a portly detective put his head inside my motor and said, "And what name are you travelling under to-night?" What was it? It began with T., and that was all I could remember.

I could not take things seriously, or think that I really was in danger; but then I remembered Red Sunday and knew all things are possible in Ireland.

CHAPTER X

THE COURT-MARTIAL

IF I HAD married a crowned head or a Cabinet Minister, I should doubtless, long ere this, have become accustomed to the presence of detectives, both inside and outside the house. As it was, the sight of one or two of these unmistakable-looking men, walking solemnly up and down the extremely respectable and old-fashioned street in London, where we waited our next summons to Ireland, was almost too much for my nerves, and sometimes for my gravity. I was alternately frightened and amused.

Somehow the big, quiet old house in which we were staying seemed centuries removed from the turmoil and horrors of present-day life in Ireland. It seemed utterly impossible that the Sinn Feiners could interfere with us here. If they did, I could imagine the butler opening the door and saying, "Not at home" in his most impressive manner, and I felt that even the most militant Sinn Feiner would retire abashed before that magisterial demeanour.

Also, of course, were my husband a royal personage or a

Minister, there would be a slight compensation in the way of emoluments. As it is, we have not even yet recovered, three months afterwards, expenses of our first trip to Ireland on Government service. Truly the wheels of H.M. Paymasters grind slowly. They also grind exceedingly small, and instead of being at all grateful to me for going over, I do not doubt that they will erase from my claim for expenses the cost of my sleeping berth and the food I consumed on the journey, and any other item which appears to them unnecessary for a mere witness.

While I waited for my summons to Ireland, I sometimes visited friends in London. On these trips, I was always asked my views on the Irish situation. I had not any to give. The situation is too complex for any one of ordinary intelligence. The only solution I can see is one of money. Cut off their trade, touch their pockets. At present Ireland is waging war and making money at one and the same time.

I know I am prejudiced: how could I be otherwise? I am not used to murder, and near at hand it was bound to make far more impression on one than a thousand tales of German atrocities.

I waited in England a month, a week over the promised time. During this time trials had already taken place in Dublin of some of the civilians involved in the attack on the Lower Mount-street house. At last, in despair, I went to the Irish Office, to see if they could find out there whether the court-martial, at which I was the principal witness, had been again postponed.

I rang the bell, and the door was opened about an inch. On explaining who I was, I was allowed to enter. Two obvious detectives sat in the hall. Each one had his hand in his right-hand coat pocket. I looked at them, and laughed outright. That particular attitude was so very familiar. The big service revolvers are usually kept there; the small automatic pistol in the left-hand breast pocket. [There was very little I did not know about revolvers. The worst of it is now, that whenever I see a man put his hand into his pocket, I always suspect a revolver, and cannot help giving an audible sigh of relief when he brings out a pipe, or some such innocent article.]

The Irish Office were sympathetic and helpful, and a date was fixed for the trial about a week later. As the time approached, I got more and more nervous. When I had first volunteered to give evidence, I had never imagined that the whole thing would not have been over in a month at most, and that one journey to Ireland would not have been sufficient.

It was now almost three months since the murders, and this was my second visit. I do not wonder that my nerves were on edge. The arrangements for this visit were also a little patchy. At one moment I was surrounded by a perfect army of detectives, officers, and military police. At others I was left severely alone.

The procession from the train to the boat at Holyhead, at the charming hour of 2 A.M., must have been a funny sight. No Customs examination now, but a special gangway.

We moved at a sharp trot, followed by the two inevitable soldiers' dogs, and precipitated ourselves on board. I was put in a cabin, and the escort piled themselves on the berths the other side of the passage, where they lay in serried rows throughout the remainder of the night. Once when I wanted some coffee, I put my head outside the door; but the moment I did so, I caused such a commotion among the ranks opposite, that I hastily withdrew it. Thank Heaven, it was a calm crossing.

This time the arrangements for meeting me were complete. At dawn and, once more, at a brisk pace, we hurried down the pier, and were distributed among the various waiting motor-cars. The one I was in was covered with wire-netting, and had other methods of defence. Anyway, it was singularly uncomfortable. It was decided that this time I was to stay in Dublin Castle. Since the court-martial would take place in the nearby City Hall, it was thought I should be safer in the Castle than at the Chief Secretary's Lodge in Phoenix Park.

The Castle is a dreadful place, surrounded by the worst slums in Dublin. Nowadays it is like a huge rabbit-warren. Every official connected in any way, however remotely, with the Government of Ireland or the police, is interned there, in many cases with their wives and families. In addition, there are innumerable military officers with their belongings, a very large number of soldiers and police. There are also scores of male and female clerks, typists, &c.

Accommodation is at a premium. Quite important people sleep two in a room - nay, two in a bed, sometimes. All day long motors dash in and out, orderlies scurry about with papers. About tea-time, lady clerks, jug in hand, wander out in search of milk, and exchange a few words of badinage with the waiting orderlies.

I had nothing whatever to do, and after walking round and round the square for an hour or so, the only form of exercise to be got, I spent the remainder of the day at the window, watching the stream of motors and passers-by on the square.

It is the gloomiest and most dreary place I have ever been in, and the only conversation ever heard is on the state of Ireland, and the latest rumours.

Some inhabitants of the Castle endeavour to lead a normal social life, if such a thing were possible in Dublin in these days. I managed to spot two intrepid warriors returning from golf. Two golf-bags were handed out of the car, and then four enormous revolvers. Another official used to sally forth, with a large escort, to lunch at his club. Alas this practice had to stop when he was asked by the other members, who considered his presence a danger, to stay away. Even the poor little children of some of the police officials never leave the Castle. Afternoon dances are held occasionally, at which the inhabitants stretch their cramped legs. It is the only exercise some of them get.

Personally it makes one ashamed to think that the Government of the most powerful Empire in the world should allow its servants to live like this, practically as prisoners in the heart of Dublin.

After doing nothing for a couple of days, the prosecuting counsel, for whom we had been waiting, arrived from England, and I was told the trial would be the next day - it was now exactly three months since the November murders.

I had never been present at even a County Court before, and I felt as if I had committed murder myself, and when I heard the well-known names of the leading English counsel, I was more nervous than ever. The next morning I waited about an hour outside the court-room, where the court-martial officer sought to cheer me up by showing me the marks on the walls of the City Hall made by the rebel bullets in 1916, and the spot where the first policeman was killed.

It was while waiting here that I heard a leading Dublin doctor say that he could stop the whole of the present trouble in half an hour. His idea was "to hang Asquith and two of his secretaries from the bridge in the centre of the town." This seemed to me a little drastic, but of course life is very cheap in Ireland, and the loyalists do not appear to like Asquith.

At last my turn came, and I was led into the presence of the Court. The Court was a most impressive sight. It was crowded with officers, and the counsel and judge-advocate in wig and gown were a strange contrast to the khaki. English and Irish law appear to be different, and there were various arguments on legal points.

On trial was the hall porter of 28 Upper Pembroke-street, who was charged with the murder, or being an accessory to the murder, of Lieutenant-Colonel Montgomery.

The prosecution claimed that the accused, who was cleaning brasses and shaking mats on that Sunday morning, allowed up to eight men into the house and to distribute themselves throughout the building to kill Lieutenant-Colonel Montgomery and other officers. There was no evidence that these men had molested the accused in any way nor did the accused appear to give any warning to the residents of the house that armed men had entered the building. After the shootings had taken place, the prosecution maintained, the accused then aided a member of the murder gang to escape by opening a rear door in the garden wall.

I was not very severely cross-examined, and the ordeal was not so bad as I had feared. It was quite easy to tell my story after all; every detail of that day is written on my heart and brain for ever.

The defending counsel sought to imply that probably, with my husband lying badly wounded, I had been nervous - too nervous, perhaps - to be quite clear as to what had really happened. But he was wrong. For one thing, I did not at first realise how badly injured my husband was, neither did I know, at first, that two other officers were dead, and three others dying, in the house. But even had I known all this, I do not think it would have made any difference. My brain was never clearer, and I never felt less nervous than I did on that morning.

In his defence, the accused maintained that he had never belonged to any political organisation, had never had any

91

charge of any kind laid before him prior to the November killings and that he had never seen any of the raiders before they had entered the house that morning.

There was also an amusing episode. One witness, called for the defence, said he had known the prisoner for years, and could testify as to his character. Counsel, wishing to emphasise the value of this witness's evidence, said, "You were a Loyalist member of the Dublin County Council, and opposed the Sinn Fein member at the last election, I think." To which the witness quickly and emphatically answered, "No, not a Loyalist, a Nationalist, sir." Not precisely the answer required.

At last the Court was closed, and, later, I heard that the prisoner had been found guilty on a lesser charge, and sentence would be promulgated later. In time, two other men were tried and convicted for their part in the November murders and were duly hanged in Mountjoy Jail several weeks after the Montgomery trial was over.

Now, at last I was free to leave Ireland for ever. But I was not to go yet without one more further shock. I sent a messenger with a telegram to the post office, a few hundred yards from the Castle. While waiting for his return, I heard that three unarmed messengers had been murdered, almost in view of the Castle gates, and I felt certain that he was one of them. It was the usual story, so common now in Ireland. A crowded street at midday, a volley of revolver shots from the usual group of loafers, not a hand raised to hinder, not a voice raised in protest; and, as usual, the assassins escaped down a side street. It was imagined that these poor men were shot "by mistake" for three others, who arrived in the street a few minutes later. Doubtless these three left mothers, widows, and children, but one never hears of these. That their men were shot "by mistake" will not be much consolation to them.

My journey back was a little uneven. Two officers were deputed to take me to London, and they duly arrived with several motors. Followed by an armoured car with machine-guns, we left for Kingstown. I could not help contrasting this with my departure from Germany, where I left with many smiles and "aufwiedersehens," carrying a large bunch of pink carnations.

As far as Holyhead all went well, but there the officials had not been told that I was coming, and no carriage had been reserved for me or my escort. I was put into a carriage marked "LADIES ONLY," and my escort left on the platform. I felt distinctly annoyed, as I compared this to my departure from Holyhead a few nights before, which had been most impressive; and I said bitterly to the detective, who had been hastily summoned by an officer, that, possibly now I had given my evidence, my life was of no further value to the authorities, but that it was still just as valuable to me, and that a label "LADIES ONLY" did not seem a very adequate protection.

Eventually I travelled with my escort in a reserved carriage. One of them unnerved me very much by placing his revolver on the seat beside him, where it was pointing straight at me. He then went to sleep, and having heard terrifying stories of how automatics went off, almost if you looked at them, I passed an anxious hour, wondering what the effect of a jolt or fall would be on the evil-looking weapon. But nothing happened. The journey seemed endless, but at last we arrived in London.

*

Shortly afterwards, I travelled to a lovely little spot in the south of France where I wanted to finish writing of my experiences in Ireland.

I unexpectedly met someone else writing his memoirs - no

less a person than M. Eleutherios Venizelos, the Greek prime minister who had recently survived an assassination bid. I inadvertently blundered into a little room reserved for him, and, as he spluttered with indignation, I fled.

Apart from such small upsets, my sojourn in France is also an opportunity to try to play a little golf. I am looking forward to another lesson from Arnaud Massey, the French champion, who kindly offered me plenty of sound advice: "Keep your eye on the ball. Do not look up. No one is going to shoot at you from behind a hedge here. You are not in Ireland!"

Thank God for that!